Highly Sensitive People Book

Use Your Emotional Intelligence to Increase Happiness and Self-Confidence, Understanding your Empathy Gift and Protecting Yourself from Other People's Negative Energy

By

Lorna Mayers

Contents

Introduction

Emotionally sensitive men and women are individuals who experience extreme emotions more often and for more extended amounts of time than many individuals do. For having picked up this book, you are probably mentally sensitive, or you know somebody who is.

Being mentally sensitive could be both a gift and a burden. If your emotions overwhelm you, then you might not see your extreme feelings as a gift. However, your caring about the others, your extreme joy, your powerful feelings of connectedness, along with your ardent nature may add a feeling of purpose, significance, and contentment for your life.

Learning how to control your extreme emotions is essential to decrease your distress and assist you to appreciate more of these psychological sensitivity gifts. Managing your emotions entails comprehending and accepting your feelings, utilizing fresh approaches to deal with uncomfortable feelings, and picking behaviors that can move your life ahead rather than shoving you deeper into insanity.

For instance, repeatedly agreeing to babysit active kids whenever you don't feel right, inviting relatives that criticize your every movement to remain in your house, shopping until you cannot pay your invoices, eating a great amount of food, and yelling at people that you love are ways you could act on feelings which make your life more difficult.

Handling your emotions is essential for living well; however, there is no path in college called Running Your Partner 101. Plus, many parents do not talk to their kids about how to manage unhappy, hurt, or upset feelings. Figuring out how to deal with strong feelings is difficult. If you ask people how they deal when they have been rejected for a project they desired or every time a beloved friend is not talking to them, then you are going to find many different answers.

Some will say that it's not a major thing and they are not concerned about it. Some will say that they simply forget about it. Most probably, you are going to be advised that time is a fantastic healer. And it is. But if you are emotionally sensitive, then these events are not small bumps in the street, and also, the pain you are feeling while awaiting the emotion to maneuver could seem unbearable.

With this book, you will learn the features of mentally sensitive men and women. You will comprehend both the general and specific tactics to handle your extreme feelings, so you're in a position to make more efficient decisions and improve your own personal and work associations.

You will practice approaches for reducing the strength of your feelings, thinking before you act, and also realizing what you are feeling. Some approaches will probably work better than others, and many will be effective after you have practiced them for a short time. Exercise is an fundamental word. Overcoming your average patterns of behavior will not be simple. Nevertheless, the human mind is much more elastic than we usually think. By learning how to deal with strong feelings, you can alter your mental habits to no longer react mechanically in ways that make the problem worse, like overeating or depriving yourself.

Chapter #1
Understanding Highly Sensitivity

If you are emotionally sensitive, your feelings tend to develop more quickly, be intense, and last longer compared to other people's feelings. You probably struggle every day to manage your feelings. You might not trust yourself since you cannot predict how you are going to respond in different scenarios.

Frequently, acting in your emotions increases distress and difficulty for your life. Individuals in your life might not know or understand the intensity of your feelings. They may feel like you're overreacting, that you're overly sensitive, or overly dramatic. You will wind up as different from other men and women, probably in a negative manner. You might dislike yourself, even despise yourself, along with the pain you're feeling.

At the same time, you might cherish being mentally sensitive. Maybe your relations with and empathy for other men and women are a source of incredible joy. You'd love to shed the debilitating feelings, but maintain your ability for relationship, compassion, and happiness. Part of figuring out how to deal with your feelings would be to comprehend the features of mentally sensitive men and women—feeling known, learning that other people share your adventures, and accepting that your psychological sensitivity will set the preparation.

Traits of Sensitive People

The majority of the characteristics of mentally sensitive individuals have an upside and a downside. Some mentally sensitive men and women encounter more of their favorable effects of being mentally sensitive, while some struggle with all the problematic effects and seldom observe the added benefits.

A Deeply Sensitive Perspective on the Natural World

For mentally sensitive people, virtually every interaction and occasion is indicated with emotion. Your powerful emotions imply you are feeling beautifully alive. At the same time, feeling these powerful emotions could be exhausting. Finding peace could be challenging. If you are emotionally sensitive, temperament may calm and ground you.

A link to nature can provide you with a feeling of belonging rather than being lonely. Smelling a blossom, hearing the sea waves, watching fall foliage, or even snuggling a puppy may replenish you once you feel tired. Emotionally sensitive individuals can also obtain a lot of relaxation from their pets and, subsequently, provide them with outstanding care. On the other side, love for nature also implies it may pain you if the creature is not respected by other people. Seeing hurt creatures can enrage you or send you to deep sadness. As a youngster, you might even worry about plants, scared that if you walk on grass, it would get hurt.

Sensitivity to Others' Emotions

Emotionally sensitive men and women are exceptionally alert to the feelings of others. If you are emotionally sensitive, sometimes you're angry, you might feel equally as mad as they perform (or more). Whenever someone needs reassurance, you likely know just what to say. When you find a person yelling, you might worry about that individual for hours. As a youngster, you might have concerns about the teacher's feelings as soon as your classmates misbehaved and concerned about your parents' finances if you had expensive supplies for college.

You are exceptionally talented in providing meaningful gifts to people. It may be a faithful ally. When a friend is crushed by life, and many others have ceased calling him, you stay by his side. When assistance is needed, you are there. The simple fact that you are acutely attuned to the others' emotions, though, can indicate that people have too much influence in your feelings. You will overanalyze people's words and behaviors and frequently be suspicious and concerned about what others think about you. You might be so worried about hurting others that you don't stand on your own sometimes. You might try to address issues for people that are in pain, even if it means giving in to their own needs if you shouldn't. You might have strong bodily responses, like an upset tummy or vomiting once you have to execute personal or business activities, which may upset the individuals involved.

Excessive Tolerance and Intolerance

The fondness that emotionally sensitive men and women feel, alongside the simple fact they're easily hurt, contributes to significant ups and downs within their relationships. If you are emotionally sensitive, then you could have a great need to get folks in your life but, in addition, you could have a responsive nature. It could be challenging to choose what's too much to endure from the others and what to avoid.

You might make excuses for people who behave poorly. Maybe you do not recognize when someone doesn't care about you, although others do, or you do not think you deserve something much better. Perhaps you believe being with somebody who's reckless is far better than being lonely. You could also respond efficiently and to little annoyances and think about ending connections over problems that would not disturb others. You can be quite cynical, even with people who are nearest to you.

You might be so doubtful that you are mad most of the time, sensing people as judgmental and unfair. Occasionally, emotionally sensitive men and women are worn out and avoid everybody.

Adhering to heartbreak and issues could be stressful and mentally fatiguing, as might being worried about how others are treating you. You will reach the stage you can't listen to a different term or only wish to be alone.

A Love/Hate Relationship with One's Own Emotions

If you are emotionally sensitive, then you are likely thankful to have extreme joy, happiness, love, and enthusiasm, in addition to the ability to associate with and care for others, and disagreeable emotions could be painful. In any particular scenario, you cannot predict how mad you will get or for how long. You do not understand when you'll be mentally overwhelmed, along with your predictions, how well you're able to deal in a variety of scenarios are often erroneous.

At times, you might wish you did not have feelings in any way. A significant concern for most emotionally sensitive individuals is that their psychological reactions can cost them important relationships. Several have lost friends, relatives, and intimate partners due to their sensitivity. You have probably pledged over and over again to control yourself.

Managing anger is very difficult. Any moment you're mad, you most likely wish to strike something. Because extreme emotions may result in misinterpretations, your anger can often be due to a mistake -- then you might attack whenever there's no reason to do so. At any moment you could strike with anger, then it endangers your relationships.

Fear of battle or inadequate conflict-resolution skills can pose additional obstacles to resolving hallucinations. You might decide you don't ever need to converse to a person again, just to regret your choice a couple of hours later. These pros and cons with people you love could be especially discouraging. You might rather stay lonely as opposed to risk the chance of losing friendships and other connections because of your emotional consequences.

Emotionally sensitive individuals frequently feel pity about being sensitive and, therefore, attempt to conceal their feelings. You might think that if you reveal your emotions, others will notice you as weak, especially if you yell easily. All these self-judgments can cause suppress your feelings, which increases the difficulty in dealing with them.

Sensitivity to Rejection

Sensitivity to rejection activates, in several different ways, using a mentally sensitive person's capability to live his life completely. Every interaction retains the chance of actual or perceived denial. If you are emotionally sensitive, then you might dread interacting due to the potential annoyance involved. Even some significant statements made from acquaintances can lead one to believe you will not ever match in.

If a friend does not include you at a luncheon invitation, then you might think you are being left out, even though you know he/she has many different friends. You may interpret a person's tone of voice as indicative that he or she does not like you. In your mind, you might think about it, fearing you mentioned something wrong, and your friends haven't forgiven you.

It might be especially unfortunate when an intimate partner does not predict you, even if you aren't sure you need to be at that level of connection. Rejection sensitivity may also make an impact on your life in different ways, like not accepting risks in college or your livelihood since you find maybe not succeeding because of rejection.

Frequent Emotional Illness

Dealing with persistent extreme feelings could be exhausting. Emotionally sensitive individuals may only spend a determined amount of time "on earth" until they will need to escape the psychological overload. If you are mentally sensitive, you might occasionally crave solitude or need to be with "safe" people to feel calm. Or maybe you find it comfortable losing yourself at a crowded location where nobody understands you. The dilemma is that you might feel pity about withdrawing and judge yourself.

Difficulty Making Decisions

If you are emotionally sensitive, then you might fight to make choices or take actions, as your extreme emotions could be paralyzing and perplexing you. You could be plagued with self-doubt. At times you might feel emotions as detailed as if you were touching an object, then it has to be authentic. Occasionally, you might respond too swiftly without considering the results. When issues are challenging to solve, you can be easily defeated and quit. You might often believe life is simply too challenging and wish you had the ability just to make decisions and proceed, as everybody else seems to do.

Intuitive Thinking

Intuition is defined as the capability to comprehend something intuitively, with no necessity for conscious rationale. Intuitive thinking is brain working in ways people are not conscious of and frequently don't know. Intuitive Individuals frequently know certain things to be authentic, though they can't explain how they attained this understanding--they just have a feeling of certainty. Emotionally sensitive men and women are usually intuitive.

You have likely experienced "intuition" that you are at risk, that somebody's lying, that somebody you have just met is the love of your life, or you should turn left at the next stoplight. You "understand" a scenario will work out alright, or someone shouldn't take a proposition, without having the ability to spell out the logic of your choice along with even the reasons you "know." Your intuitive thinking may be an essential source; however, your powerful emotions may hinder using it. For instance, anxious folks can be especially attuned with their partner's negative emotions and ideas and not as conscious of their positive ones. Getting attuned to this negativity clearly, will highlight your image of their connection. Learning how to use your instinct can consequently be quite a challenge.

Creativity

There are a lot of methods for being imaginative. If you are emotionally sensitive, then you might be artistic, exceptionally gifted, a superb author, or gifted at the interior layout. You will create attractive flower arrangements or appealing outfits. Maybe you've got a brilliant imagination or throw fantastic parties. If you are emotionally sensitive, you might be especially great at seeing the "greater picture." You will show the opportunity to put things together in odd ways or to observe how making certain modifications could cause something brand new --which means you frequently arrive to novel solutions to issues. These abilities might serve you in the company world, where original solutions are appreciated. As an instance, you might easily find out how a quicker method of cleaning the floor might be successfully promoted as a means for parents to raise the time that they need to improve their kids' school performance or to get an individual to impress a vital mother-in-law.

A Powerful Sense of Justice

Emotionally sensitive men and women are attentive about injustice if it impacts them or not. They are upset when they view activities they believe are not honest, and they are prepared to endure to the person they believe was wronged. Sometimes this could lead to a mentally sensitive individual fighting battles for many others that those folks would need to struggle for themselves. For instance, if you are emotionally sensitive, then perhaps you've called your kid's college to inform it that he shouldn't be relied upon because his brother had been the person who left him late. Though others may see your attempts to make life to safeguard people as commanding or overinvolved, you do not see how anybody can let injustices occur without needing a standalone.

A Fluid Identity

Your own identity is the comprehension of what you are as an individual. It comprises your preferences, your worth, and also your personality traits. Intense feelings can hinder knowing who you are and creating a core group of values that function as a manual for living your life. Emotionally sensitive men and women can feel adrift in life, pushed here and there by what's on their way. One mentally sensitive person explained to me this way: "I am not certain

who I'm; occasionally, I am who I want to be for this circumstance."
Other folks say, "I am still attempting to find myself" and "I believe
I tend to flip-flop. I attempt to be what others need before the actual
me becomes imperceptible."

Because emotions offer you essential details regarding your identity,
it is important to experience and handle them. If you do not allow
yourself to feel emotion, then you will not get the essential feedback
to assess exactly what you like and dislike correctly. If, on the other
hand, your feelings are overpowering, it could be tough to hear just
what they're telling you. With no good identity, your awareness of
how you can change based on who you are with, what publication
you see, or wherever you're. Just like a chameleon, you switch to
match with people around you. On a single day, you might make
confident you're an environmentalist who would like to stay off the
property. But a week after, you might be enthusiastic about
committing yourself to a spiritual cause.

Developing Emotional Sensitivity

For years, people have debated whether individual behavior and
personality traits are more caused by experience or genetics. The
overall notion --no surprise --is both your surroundings or life
experiences result in your nature and your ability to handle your
emotions. To put it differently, your life experiences, such as your
family's reactions and actions and interactional styles, in addition to

the ones of other significant individuals in your life, either contribute to or reduce your difficulty in dealing with extreme feelings.

It isn't to mention that if you are emotionally sensitive, then you should have grown up within an exhibition surrounding. But if your psychological sensitivity wasn't approved and not known on your household -- maybe your caretakers disregarded your psychological sensitivity or they responded critically or perhaps abusively--you might have certain difficulty accepting and handling your emotions.

The Hurricane Rating Scale of Emotional Sensitivity

Being mentally sensitive and using difficult emotions does not mean that you're basically different from anybody else. Instead, consider becoming mentally sensitive as residing within a hurricane, whose intensity varies based on how sensitive you're. At the end of this scale (class 1) are the people that are somewhat more sensitive compared to the vast majority of individuals. These people today experience markedly enhanced psychological intensity but minimum harm to their relationships and life objectives.

Individuals in the center of this scale (class 3) reside with embarrassing intensity and harm to the stable elements of their own lives, like new connections, industry interactions, and some other action that creates stress (e.g., attending faculty).

At the end of this scale (class 5) are people who will be the most mentally sensitive, for whom feelings are always overwhelming and cause significant harm to the majority of sections of the own lives, such as family relationships, friendships, along with their capacity to operate on daily basis.

You must have any notion of where you're in this scale, since if you reside with class 5 or 4 psychological sensitivity (i.e., even if you ranked as "firmly emotionally sensitive" about the self-assessment from the introduction for this book), you will want to be active in utilizing your working abilities than those who are somewhat less sensitive.

Psychological Disorders and Emotional Sensitivity

For reasons which aren't apparent, some men and women that are born with psychological sensitivity and also have stressful life situations do not develop psychological, disposition, or even behavioral disorders, but some do. Some mentally sensitive individuals have implied an extreme interest, such as studying, or even a connection with a supportive adult, including a buddy, parent, grandparent, or even instructor, significantly enhanced their capacity to adapt to life. If you have a diagnosis of depression, nervousness, BPD, or a different ailment that reflects difficulty handling feelings, treatment of the identification is of primary concern.

Nineteen studies are demonstrating that psychotherapy affects brain functioning in a certain way for individuals with acute depression, post-traumatic anxiety disease, obsessive-compulsive disease, anxiety disorder, social anxiety disorder, specific phobias, and BPD.

Although this book is not about the therapy of those ailments and is not meant to substitute treatment, the working skills it trains may nonetheless be valuable to you. If you are now in treatment, talk about the ideas introduced in this book with your therapist before attempting them. If you have completed treatment for psychological illness, the thoughts in this book might be beneficial in further decreasing your psychological pain.

Putting It All Together

Being mentally sensitive may be equally your best gift and your hardestbest challenge. Sometimes it's difficult to enjoy the advantages of psychological

sensitivity, as experiencing feelings so intensely could be debilitating and cause severe conditions. The upcoming steps in learning how to handle your feelings so they don't overwhelm you will examine how your sensitivity impacts your life and learn a few simple emotion management abilities.

Chapter #2
Reclaiming Control

Logical thinking can be regarded as an indication of maturity and intellect. If you are emotionally sensitive, then needing to stay up to this standard of wisdom and maturity may enhance your difficulty in engaging and dealing with your own emotions, as your emotions frequently overwhelm your logic. Perhaps you feel that life could be simpler without despair, jealousy, or fear--then you would not need to suffer the looks that you get from the others if you cry as you are mad, or people would not shake their heads like you had been a kid when you wonder why your neighbor did not say hi this morning. Life without feelings can seem quite attractive.

But, emotions deliver significant advice for living life in a secure and gratifying manner. For instance, fear informs you when to run out of danger. Adore suggests who to safeguard and develop a connection with, and pleasure enhances your ability to appreciate favorable encounters. Your emotions can also be an important source of inspiration. You do not wish to waste time organizing your escape when a hungry tiger is assaulting you--you would like to conduct. Emotion, not logic, prompts one to assist the poor and many others in the issue. Logic is not why someone jumps to some freezing-cold lake to rescue a kid from drowning. A fantastic method for making everyday choices, therefore, would be to utilize logical thinking together with input from your own emotions.

Maintaining your feelings and the information that they communicate will be able to assist you in making better decisions. Section of expressing your emotions always knows the style where you communicate them.

Kinds of Emotional Illness

Emotional sensitivity could be obvious in two different ways: psychological reactivity and psychological avoidance. Although I will clarify these patterns of behavior individually, maybe you go back and forth or have been somewhere in the center. Occasionally, your behavior may be based on the circumstance.

Emotional Reactivity

If you are normally emotionally responsive, you act in your feelings without thinking. You mix anger, despair, joy, enthusiasm, and also other emotions together with gusto. You will jump onto a plane to see a friend though you do not have the money to spare. You are the person who begins the line and sing-alongs at parties. If your boss does not accept your request for a holiday, you are going to send her an upset email. If you discover a text out of a woman in your husband's telephone, you may just throw his clothes out on the yard. However, the following day, once you're calmer and comprehend

19

that the note was naive, you will text him a hundred times to apologize.

When you are emotionally responsive, controlling the cravings, which include powerful emotions, is hard. In the instant that you write that mad email to a boss, you do not care you might be dismissed. When you ditch your spouse's clothes in the yard, you do not believe there could be a justification, like the notice was out of his secretary about a consultation that he had with a client.

At that moment, your emotions let you know that the action is suitable. But then you are ashamed of your behavior. You guarantee yourself, "Never again, not again," however, you constantly do it. For emotionally responsive folks, the main step toward diminishing insanity will be to postpone acting on urges. You need methods to calm your feelings so you are able to think more clearly and then make a decision as to what activities will be most effective. Mindfulness is a superb approach to come up with a delay between the impulse to get something and actually doing this. Calming techniques mentioned later in this phase may also be useful.

Emotional Avoidance

If you are normally emotionally avoidant, then you do not want to confront uncomfortable feelings or situations which cause them. Avoiding painful feelings altogether may appear to be a fantastic idea. You may numb your feelings through over-exercising, overeating, and so on. Or maybe you push your emotions off, so you are not conscious of these, possibly so fast you do not even recognize they occured. Not setting your emotions requires a great deal of energy, and that means you are probably tired a lot at the moment.

In reality, a surprising sense of fatigue might be a signal that you are pushing off emotions. Perhaps you're conscious of your emotions but wear a mask for some other men and women. You maintain your smile in position and do not admit even minor pops. You state things like, "I am fine--what is wrong?" You may say anger to conceal other emotions, such as sadness, which forces you to feel much more vulnerable.

Mindfulness may boost your perception of negative feelings so you can develop methods of dealing with them. Taking measures to identify your own emotions, like analyzing your bodily senses, exploring your urges to behave, and discovering the reason, can help you create effective methods for reacting to your emotions where you behave on the info they supply. If you typically prevent your feelings, then you might be tempted to bypass the exercises in this book. Instead, finish them to help you understand not only the data but also conquer your avoidance.

CHASING GOOD FEELINGS

In general, psychological avoidance includes the pursuit of feeling good or preventing pain in the short run, even if the long-term effects are harmful. Preventing difficult emotions by following a feel-good agenda does not usually get the job done. You will always chase joy yet not locate it. Consider how, after having a cupcake, you might believe that ingesting a different cupcake will be quite as wonderful. Nevertheless, the true experience of eating another dessert is not very likely to genuinely make you happier. You will drink more coffee, purchase more clothing, and remain in to get a new cellphone, though you already have those items. A good deal of craving and desires really leads to unhappiness. Allowing your urges to overeat, overdrink, overspend, or attempt to feel great (and prevent complicated feelings) can be hard. A very first step would be to get a strategy for what you will do if you've to engage in behavior that is not valuable. Write out your strategy. Locate a productive replacement behavior like practice, playing games with friends, or phoning friends for assistance.

Another choice is to compose numerous reasons not to participate in the behavior. Keep this list on you, and see if you are tempted to pursue these actions, which will enhance your distress in the long run. Some people today carry an item like a rock, a necklace using a logo, or another piece of jewelry to remind them about the commitment to not engage in false extra-curricular pursuits. If you discover you are unable to quit, then think about seeking skilled assistance or attending 12-step meetings. Maybe a part of the motivation to pursue fantastic emotions is that you are fearful of feelings. You might have developed a strain of some or all your feelings and be nervous at the very first indication of feelings.

EMOTION PHOBIA

There are lots of reasons why you might have developed a strain of your feelings. Maybe when you were younger, then your caretakers penalized you badly when you voiced a particular emotion, like anger. You might have discovered that having feelings is "incorrect." Perhaps you're fearful of despair since you have endured deep depression and anxiety that you will relapse if you are sad.

You will be afraid to be out of control once you are emotional. No matter the reason, you fear when you encounter stressing feelings. You might feel stressed or have the temptation to flee at the first sign you experience the feelings that frighten you. Your anxiety could come on so fast you don't have any consciousness of the emotion which triggered it and know only of becoming overwhelmed with stress. Overcoming anxiety about your emotions involves permitting them to encounter them. Only by experiencing them you will understand they will not last forever, and you may tolerate them. Seeking help from a therapist is very likely to be significant in this circumstance.

Being Overwhelmed by Emotions Affects Your Life

Whether you still are inclined to be emotionally responsive, mentally avoidant, or even one and sometimes the other, then your own emotions change your life in several different ways. The following form will direct you in analyzing the manners your extreme feelings have aided and hindered you in different moments of your life.

You might locate this exercise mentally debilitating to finish. Have somebody close by for assistance or create plans to perform a task after that you have completed it. It will require your focus, for example, having dinner with a buddy or exercising. The action should be one that may divert you from disturbing thoughts. Identifying the reasons to change (in this scenario, to boost your working abilities) is part of a successful shift.

The feelings you will experience from performing the exercise will probably be temporary. But if there is any irreparable injury previously, or if you have some reason to think this exercise may greatly disturb you, then take action just with the consent or assistance of a therapist.

The Price and Benefits of Your Mental Intensity

For each of these categories, compose different manners being mentally sensitive has helped and hindered you. The way your emotions have taken advantage over you might not be instantly evident. Still, if you think carefully, you're probably going to discover that your emotions have added meaning to your life in significant ways.

Romantic Relationships, Marriage

How has being mentally sensitive assisted you in this region?

_____

How has it disturbed you? _____

Work

How has being mentally sensitive assisted you in this region?

_____

How has it disturbed you? _____

Parenting

How has being mentally sensitive assisted you in this region?

_____

How has it disturbed you? _____

Life Dreams

How has being mentally sensitive assisted you in this region?

_____

How has it disturbed you? _____

Friendships

How has being mentally sensitive assisted you in this region?

_____

How has it disturbed you? _____

Social Activities

How has being mentally sensitive assisted you in this region?

_____

How has it disturbed you? _____

Leisure Time, Hobbies

How has being mentally sensitive assisted you in this region?

_____

How has it disturbed you? _____

Spiritual Life

How has being mentally sensitive assisted you in this region? _____

How has it disturbed you? _____

Now think about any patterns that you see on your answers. Do your extreme feelings affect you or benefit you at precisely the very same manners in every single category? What exactly do you really wish to change? As an instance, maybe you often become frustrated and concentrate on jobs you dedicated to finishing, and you also wish to have the ability to keep everything together. Learning how to deal efficiently with discouragement is among your objectives.

Next, you are going to examine the specifics of how you communicate your feelings. Understanding your typical behaviors when you've got particular emotions can allow you to speak more clearly. Identifying your emotional reaction patterns can allow you to change the routines which are not great or even healthy.

Your Emotions and Behaviours

During the next week or two, if you encounter among the recorded emotions, first rate the degree of the emotion on a scale of 1 to 5, where 1 = moderate and five = very extreme. Then write what you did if you felt like that. For instance, if you felt unhappy, you might

27

have cried. Or you might have spoken with friends, overeaten, gone shopping, or even pushed away from the feeling.

Regardless of what you do with your emotions, then you probably have expectations for what can occur. If you are sad, for instance, based on what you do, you might expect you could steer clear of the despair, not feel alone, forget about everything made you depressed, locate a person to listen to you, or perhaps alter the circumstance. If you overate if you're miserable, perhaps you concentrated on feeling better in the short run and disregarded how you may feel in the very long term. Write what you're expecting would occur when you did everything you did.

From the column labeled "Actual Outcomes," clarify what occurred in either the short and the long run. Things could have gone just as you anticipated, or else they might have gone differently. For instance, perhaps you desired or anticipated your buddy to inquire what was wrong when you hauled in anger, and what which occurred is that he/she dismissed you.

Attempt to list all of this info as soon as possible following the encounter. The more quickly you get it done, the more precise and useful the info will likely be.

Emotion	Intensity	What You Did	What You Were Expecting	Actual Results
Sadness				
Anger				
Jealousy				
Frustration				
Fear				
Love				
Shame				
Rejection				

After the graph is full (or almost complete), examine what you've written for every emotion. Notice patterns in how your emotions influence your behavior. Some behaviors might help you get what you would like, though some may hinder you from living your life the way you wish to live it.

Are you doing precisely the same behavior repeatedly in reaction to a particular emotion though it is not beneficial or powerful and perhaps even has undesirable outcomes? Do your activities change at a specific amount of emotional strength?

Keep what you heard in the previous exercises in mind while you find out more about the necessary abilities for handling your own emotions. You can replace the behaviors that are not functioning well for you with much more skillful behaviors.

First Step to Control: Emotional First Aid

You have probably discovered by now that if you are full of emotion, you frequently don't act in logical ways, and the outcomes of your activities are not pleasant in the very long term. That is very likely to be no real surprise. Perhaps you've assured yourself several times that your feelings wouldn't control you.

You might believe the challenge is a lack of willpower to stick with everything you stated you were planning to do. But everybody's willpower is restricted -- you just have a lot. You will keep to a guarantee to get a couple of hours or even days, after which your emotions will probably overwhelm you. Willpower does not get the job done. Employing sheer willpower, averting your feelings, and pursuing approaches to feel better can make you miserable and more helpless in the very long term.

You probably already know a few of the approaches which do work, but you're not using them. When you feel that your activities are out of control, it is difficult for you to take actions that create a difference. These techniques can allow you to feel less helpless in general. In subsequent chapters, you will find out more detailed approaches. Keep in mind, only knowing the approaches does not work--you must exercise and utilize them.

Identify the Reason

If you are emotionally sensitive, then you often are uncertain about the motives for your own emotions. You might sometimes discover that you are depressed, fearful, or angry but do not understand why. If you're able to identify what you are feeling and the origin accurately, then you will better understand how to deal efficiently.

For instance, if you are afraid as a snowstorm is coming, then stocking up on food and putting snow tires on your automobile are practical and logical actions to take. Taking proper action to resolve or make a difference regarding the issue can allow you to handle the emotion. From time to time, however, there are no actions you can take. If you understand you are worried because somebody you love is having minor surgery tomorrow, there's nothing you can do to alter the circumstance. Still, you may bear in mind that the rationale behind your angry is time-restricted.

By knowing that you will simply need to deal with that stress temporarily, it is possible to discover ways to comfort or distract yourself. Now imagine that you are anxious but have not thought about the rationale. Then you go through your entire week feeling uneasy. Eventually, you think about what may be causing your distress. You see you haven't learned from the business at which you applied for a job a week ago.

It can help you place the emotion in outlook. You might grin and shake your mind, realizing that if you want the occupation, it would not be bad if you did not get it. Identifying the rationale behind your emotion makes it possible to handle the emotion differently in cases like this. From time to time, emotionally sensitive men and women state the main reason behind their madness is that actually terrible things do happen in the world. As an example, this idea adds on to their distress.

But overall, ideas like this one are frequently the result of feeling depressed or harmed. This is opposed to finding the origin of the distress. Start looking for specific events that resulted in worldwide judgment. If you believe your life is a wreck, what's the latest illustration of your life becoming a wreck? Thorough, factual statements, such

as "My mother said she had been upset and fed up because I asked her for cash again," will aid you in finding answers to difficulties. General announcements of distress, for example, "My mother's a greedy jerk," will just lead one to feel helpless and hopeless.

Connecting the Emotion with the Cause

During the next week, see when you encounter a powerful emotion.

Every moment, complete the next form. Emotion you are experiencing: _____

Event that triggered the emotion (be specific): _____

Can you resolve or decrease the issue? Is there some activity to take?

_____

If the issue cannot be readily solved, however, can be time-limited, just how do you comfort or distract yourself? _____

When you have completed this workout for each week, you might discover that it's somewhat simpler to link your emotions with their triggers. You will get a clearer idea of how to deal effectively when you understand the origin of any specific emotion.

Understand Your Feelings Are Not Necessarily Truth

If you are feeling happy and comfortable, you typically have positive thoughts and, most importantly, the whole world feels right to you. If you are angry, you might not recall how great you felt earlier and not be able to feel you might feel great again, though nothing else on your life has significantly altered. During these occasions, your ideas tend to be bleak, and you might observe all as impossible.

Ideas like "I feel unhappy because the entire world is a dreadful place, and my life is a wreck" could possibly be normal. That is just the way that the human mind works. You tend to find the world according to your own emotions at a specified moment. For mentally sensitive folks, this may make an emotional roller coaster ride in which one day you are up, and the following day you are down.

One approach to give up your distress indefinitely is to monitor your feelings. Keep a journal where you write on your emotions as well as the events that occurred daily. After a month or two, return and examine what you've written. You will realize your prognosis will change along with your feelings. Recognizing your ideas frequently reflect your emotions, and not always the truth of your life can be useful.

Do Not Feed Painful Emotions

It might appear plausible that handling difficult emotions, such as sadness, entails not doing things that add to all those feelings or make them more powerful. Nonetheless, this is more difficult than it seems. If you are depressed, you likely won't opt to be around happy men and women that are laughing. You are very likely to look for others that are miserable.

If you are mad with somebody, you might think of reasons to be upset about this individual, with the consequence that you remain mad more. If you have just broken up with your intimate partner, you're going to be attracted to sad songs about lost love. The fantastic news is that there are several ways in which you are able to keep yourself out of making difficult feelings much more extreme.

STOP THE REPLAY

When you are angry or fearful or undergoing other embarrassing feelings, you might repeatedly replay in mind whatever happened to cause you to think that way. You might search for further proof to back up how you feel, perhaps to justify your own emotions. You might remember all of the wrongs individuals have done to you personally, each of the times if a specific individual was unlucky or each of the errors you have made.

This behavior is so common there is a word for this "throwing into the kitchen sink." Creating a record of past wrongs does not help solve the present scenario, yet --it just makes you upset. One approach to quit reigniting your feelings would be to remind yourself to remain in the here and now. Concentrate just on the present scenario, and if your brain goes adrift, softly refocus your attention--and again, if you will need to (see chapter 4 for further specifics).

You may also try the subsequent casual mindfulness practice: Notice your ideas about previous encounters that made you mad. Subsequently, notice whether the ideas are useful. Explain the notions as such--state for yourself, that is a beneficial notion, or that idea is not valuable. Another choice is to practice approval.

Accepting what happened does not mean that you approve or agree to what exactly occurred. Accepting what occurred signifies that you that admit it happened. You quit wishing it had been different, presuming it shouldn't have occurred or endangering others, and take that it did occur, and it is finished. Acceptance can be about your thoughts. Accepting that you are with an upsetting idea implies that you quit fighting with the notion. Every time you have the idea, you tag it "That is a notion"--and then prevent yourself from moving down the "what if" route. By doing this, you recognize that simply because you believe something does not mean it is true. People have ideas all of the time that do not represent reality.

A number of our ideas are all about matters which are out of their hands. It is also possible to substitute other ideas to prevent an unhelpful inspection of the upsetting situation. Counting backward in a hundred from threes or performing multiplication tables within the mind, as an instance, can be useful.

ABANDON EMOTIONAL REASONING

As soon as your emotions are extreme, it's easy to trust the ideas that follow them. These ideas are called psychological rationale. Sometimes only experiencing anxiety or other troubling emotions direct you to be sure something awful has to occur or will happen due to your feeling. For instance, if you are afraid you will fail your exam, you might have the idea "I am sure I will fail my evaluation". Or if you fear something is wrong with your wellbeing, you might believe "I must be sick indeed."

Considering such a mentally created "reality" about what is going to take place or what really did occur can make the problem worse. For instance, if you get in the idea: "I am sure I will fail my evaluation" depending on the feeling you have, you might prevent taking the exam or studying for this since it appears useless. So you damage or forfeit your odds of actually passing this exam.

If you think the idea "I must really be sick", you might avoid visiting a doctor since you would rather never know exactly how awful it really is. If this is so, any health issue you've, could be severe and more difficult to deal with. In addition, you forgo the odds that the physician would tell you you're not sick and consequently end your continuous anxiety. Emotions supply you with advice, but occasionally that info can be researched.

Emotional reasoning maybe just like a false alert. You could worry about the result of your clinical evaluations; however, the emotion does not signify that the result is doomed. Feeling apprehensive about a job interview does not indicate that you are not likely to find the job. Emotional justification is different from instinct. When you are using your instinct, there is a calm feeling of understanding.

You only know something is accurate, despite the fact that you cannot articulate, and there is minimal emotion connected with that understanding. When you are using psychological reasoning, you are often bloated and distressed. Deciding whether you are responding to instinctive knowledge or psychological reasoning is vital. If you are responding to psychological rationale, then admit your ideas are based on your own emotions rather than on truth. Try out the breathing exercises, comfort exercises, and other thoughts in this chapter to help lessen the uneasy feeling.

Take a Rest

If you are experiencing uncomfortable emotions, like fear or anger, you most likely wish to settle the problem whenever possible. Instead, practice getting a rest until you are calm, to ensure your logical thinking will arise. Everything you do during this fracture is vital. Some activities can allow you to handle your feelings effectively, along with other activities, will raise your psychological upset. Below are a few recommendations.

Breathing Exercises. Your body will be stressed once you're mentally upset. Just slowing your exhalations is really a method of quieting yourself. One means to do so is to breathe from a count of seven. Breathe through your nose and out through your mouth, pursing your lips, puffing your lips and creating a blowing noise. It's possible to add to the exercise by restricting while breathing as well. Whatever amount you use for breathing outside, breathe for half that amount. For instance, if you breathe out to a count of seven, then breathe in for a count of four. Repeat four times. Repeat one or two times per day, along with any time you are upset.

Visualization or Guided Imagery. Visualization is a method of coping with your imagination to envision relaxing occasions. Guided visualization or guided imagery is whenever someone tells you exactly what to envision, frequently in a movie or sound recording.

Individuals frequently participate in visualization to lessen their tension or maybe to assist themselves prevent heading over bothering events within their minds. You may want to picture all of your difficulties being removed.

For instance, envision your troubling ideas being packaged by employing a metal case that you lock and chain. Subsequently, envision putting the situation at the base of a bottomless pit and then covering it with concrete. Or you may want to imagine being in a relaxing location, like in the next example. Get in a comfortable place. Breathe deeply and slowly in and out. Keep this breathing. Feel the atmosphere input your entire body and texture have as you discharge them.

As you launch your breath, then notice the way the muscles in your face relax. Feel yourself becoming heavier and thicker. Now in time, you've nowhere to go, nothing else to do. Concentrate on your breath as you breathe in and out and relaxing your muscles. Picture yourself walking toward a long, sandy shore. The sand is nearly pure white, warm, and soft beneath your bare toes. The air smells somewhat salty and wash.

As you get nearer to the sea, you observe the vivid blue water is crystal clear. Shells of all sizes and shapes glisten on the coastline or twinkle under the waves. You stand where you're to get a few minutes, simply seeing and listening to the surf. The sun feels warm on the skin, and there is not one cloud in the skies.

A gentle breeze blows off, leaving tiny drops of ocean spray in your arms and face. Sometimes you listen to the far-off high-pitched cry of a gull. After a time, you observe a grove of palm trees a brief distance off, surrounded by tropical blossoms. You wander over to smell the blossoms, and you find a hammock strung between two of those palm trees. You climb in the hammock, resting your head on the pillow that is there. You lie, listening to the waves coming into and going out, over and above. You breathe in and out, let go of stress.

Produce Your Visualization

Making growing more private can help it become even more successful. Perhaps you would rather have a cottage in the hills than ashore. Maybe certain sounds or scents are especially comforting for you. To assist you in developing ideas for your customized visualization, then follow these directions, composing your answers.

1. Describe your favorite way to unwind.
2. Describe in detail the relaxing things to view.
3. Describe in detail the relaxing things to smell.
4. Describe in detail the relaxing things to contact base.
5. Describe in detail the relaxing location. Include the best way to encounter this place concerning all of your senses.
6. Describe in detail some individuals that you need to have in your visualization.
7. Can you rather walk around or remain still on your visualization?

Currently, weave all of the above into a visualization story. If your favorite smell is apple pie, for instance, you can get that smell floating with you regardless of where your favorite area is. As soon as you've written out the visualization, then have a friend record it to you personally or listing yourself. Keep it on your telephone or a different device in which you have ready access to it.

Progressive Muscle Relaxation. Progressive muscle relaxation reduces muscular tension and reduces your stress level. In this method, you essentially stress bands of muscles as you breathe and relax them as you breathe. You do that beginning with the toes, go along with your feet or calves, and work your way up for your face. Progressive muscle relaxation can help lessen stress, also helps with insomnia.

Distraction. At times the perfect approach to calm your self is to divert yourself out of whatever is bothering you. Don't forget to allow yourself to feel all those emotions exist before using diversion. Feeling the feelings is essential, so you receive the advice your emotions are providing you, and you are not using diversion as prevention. But continued to feel extreme emotions through the years could be exhausting, and you need to have methods to take breaks out of the feelings. Perhaps you're able to perform a game, see a film, or phone a buddy to talk about other subjects. The diversion will not remove the debilitating feelings, but it will help you endure them until the situation moves or your emotions decrease in strength.

Reset. Occasionally it can be difficult to allow a sense to go. Finding methods to "reset" yourself mentally can provide help. The old expression that "things will probably seem better in the daytime" is frequently accurate. If little else works, go to sleep if you're able to. You will probably wake up less psychologically upset. Exercise is very good for decreasing your nervousness and quieting your emotions, so you are able to think more clearly. Any exercise which raises your heart rate should get the job done. Altering up your body temperature may also be useful. Showering with warm water going for a stroll in cold weather may be a fantastic strategy. Occasionally only laughing out loud--a lengthy, deep belly laugh--may function to reduce your psychological anguish. If this is so, you are able to keep funny movies available, or merely throw yourself in laughing.

Understand the Greater Picture

Your feelings might blind one to details about situations or people who don't encourage the feelings you are experiencing right now. When you are mad to somebody, as an instance, it's unlikely you will think of all of the times that the individual was helpful or kind.

Anger frees your eyesight so that everything you notice is how dreadful the other individual is and just how much you despise him. For instance, let us say that your wife forgot to find last-minute groceries, which you will need to get a party you are hosting within one hour. Most probably, you're going to be mad and remember the rest of the times she had not come through, forgetting those occasions when she had been kind or helpful. If it is possible to push

43

yourself to consider the times your partner has been supportive, then you will have a more balanced and accurate opinion. Look at writing a list of the ways that the men and women in your life help you and assist you. Keep the list at hand. If you are feeling mad or upset with them, browse the list to help you maintain the "great picture" in your mind.

Produce a Different Emotion

Occasionally handling your emotions means making a different emotion, even one that is more agreeable. Especially when an emotion has been taking a very long time to dissipate, and the situation does not appear to match together with the strength of your emotions (i.e. you are not certain why you are feeling like this). It might be useful to take part in a task that makes the contrary emotion into what you feel. If you are anxious or depressed, for instance, it could be helpful to see a series that makes you laugh. If you are mad, consider seeing a scary film. Discussing or just considering people that you adore (or that adore you) can also do the job. Focusing on empathy toward someone who you're angry with may also alter your own emotion.

Believe Now and Here

Sometimes when you are overwhelmed by emotion, it is because you are considering the long run. You could be thinking about how you will ever receive a college diploma when you are still taking trainee classes or the way you are ever going to get transferred into a new house when you've only just begun appearing. Perhaps you're telling yourself there is no way possible to get through the remainder of the week. To assist you getting a little perspective on the circumstance, imagine how it might be like for your young kid reading a school textbook. You might be readily overwhelmed whenever you consider the final scope.

On the flip side, if you believe just about everything you have to do today, you can handle it. Perhaps everyday events frequently lead you to get overwhelming thoughts and emotions, like "How can I get during the afternoon then insult my sister?" The solution remains the same: concentrate on your immediate next actions. If your next job would be to visit the supermarket, simply concentrate on getting at the vehicle, then concentrate on driving into the shop, then focus on every item in your supermarket. Doing just what you have to do at the present time will reduce your awareness of being overrun.

Let Yourself Cry

If you are emotionally sensitive, then you might be especially vulnerable to rips. You're very likely to fret about what yelling may mean about your character. Maybe people tell you that you shout "all of the time," and you evaluate yourself as an outcome.

You will see crying as an indication of weakness. Yet crying is a method of coping with powerful feelings. There are great reasons to shout.

To begin with, crying is regarded as a concerted behavior --a behavior intended to ease peace and friendship instead of adversity. Crying signs to other people, you don't need to battle. (In the end, you cannot actually fight nicely with tears flowing out of your eyes) Secondly, crying signals a willingness to become exposed to relationships, and it is an essential part of familiarity. Crying reveals others your walls come down and you are undefended. It is a profound chance for you and a different individual to grow closer.

This way, crying will help you construct intimate relationships, which will hopefully give rise to a life of bliss. Third, crying is generally an effective way of getting help or relaxation, since most folks have an urge to provide comfort or help to somebody who's crying. Yelling is universally known as an indication of distress. On the contrary, crying is a means to communicate different emotions. Individuals may laugh until they cry. They shout for pleasure, in addition to fear, sorrow, and despair.

Many people today shout when they are angry. At times you might end up yelling because of overpowering feelings you can't put into words.

Ultimately, crying might help you calm yourself. Compounds released on your tears in addition to one mind can help you feel better after yelling. Allowing yourself to yell may be a positive working ability.

Practicing Emotional First Aid

Practice the skills addressed in this chapter weekly. Exercise if you are not angry, in addition to if you're. Then write the way you used every ability and outline in what manner it worked or did not get the job done. You could realize that practising for a few more weeks, even while continuing to see this publication, can further reinforce your skills. You might also wish to return to the workout (and many others) after you have finished the book.

Identifying the Cause

The way you used this ability: _____

Just how it worked: _____

Not Feeding Painful Emotions

The way you used this ability: _____

Just how it worked: _____

Taking a Break

The way you used this ability: _____

Just how it worked: _____

Assessing the Great Picture

The way you used this ability: _____

Just how it worked: _____

Developing a Different Emotion

The way you used this ability: _____

Just how it worked: _____

Thinking Now and Here

The way you used this ability: _____

Just how it worked: _____

Allowing Yourself Cry

The way you used this ability: _____

Just how it worked: _____

Putting It All Together

Emotions may overwhelm your perception to the stage in which you behave in a way that detours you in the life you would like to contribute. Paying attention to understanding your emotional reaction patterns and the way they impact your life could be embarrassing. Still, it is going to help you understand what you have to do to handle your own emotions. Within this chapter, you learned several overall coping strategies. From the chapter ahead, we will get more specific about how to handle your own emotions efficiently.

Chapter #3
Basics Make a Difference

You probably already know you should have enough exercise and sleep. You have likely heard it from your mom, from the physician, in magazine articles, also in wellness news reports. But were you aware that practicing these fundamental thoughts, really living them daily, can enhance your ability to handle your feelings? Most of us have less psychological control once we're ill, tired, exhausted, or hungry. And if you are emotionally sensitive, then you're going to be overwhelmed with your feelings more than others under similar circumstances; therefore, it is particularly important to look after yourself. Overwhelming emotions frequently get in the sense of not just having a healthy daily routine, like getting regular exercise and sleep, but also staying organized. Taking the time to really take care of your physical wellness and arrange your surroundings, not simply intellectually knowing the significance of doing this will enhance your life longer than you may imagine.

<u>Sleep</u>

Adequate sleep aids your mind work effectively in several ways. To begin with, the time spent sleeping is the sole opportunity for the own adrenal gland to rest and recover. This region of your mind, right on your brow, is thought to help you keep control of your own emotions, assess situations, and forecast. That is very likely to occur if you choose certain activities, like quitting your job or ridding your buddy for preventing you. To put it differently, your adrenal gland does all the difficult job of earning good choices. Whether you are resting on the beach, reading a fantastic book, or even listening to music, then your prefrontal cortex is functioning. It is always working out, except when you are sleeping.

Secondly, through sleep, your mind can locate connections and create relationships between thoughts. If you've got a problem you don't understand the solution to, have a fantastic night's sleep then you might arrive at the answer. Perhaps you'll wake up with only the ideal term for the song you are writing or a good idea of how to arrange the carpool program. At length, sleep can bring about greater tolerance for migraines, improved problem-solving abilities, higher understanding of social issues, and emotional flexibility. For instance, you will probably find you are more aware of different people's perspectives and much more able to accommodate changes in your program if you have a fantastic night's sleep.

Whenever You Don't Get a Good Night's Sleep

If you are emotionally sensitive, then your emotions can make it difficult to find the rest you want. You will be worried so much you have difficulty falling asleep, and wake up too early and cannot return to sleep, or even wake up during the evening. Deficiency of adequate sleep will indicate you are going to have more difficulty handling your feelings and producing successful decisions.

You will respond faster and with much more extreme feelings to smaller difficulties if you are tired. Whenever you don't sleep enough, you might encounter memory problems, concentration and attention issues, and diminished work-related skills. You lose your capacity to comprehend the significance of new info, along with your thinking, becomes stiffer. Deficiency of sleep may diminish your sense of confidence and, and this may evolve into melancholy. Your anxiety threshold is reduced when you do not get sufficient sleep, which means that routine tasks might appear overwhelming and tiny irritations may trickle to large ones. Transferring a half-mile into the shop for milk may look like an excessive amount of work. Effectively responding to a crying child in the supermarket may appear hopeless.

Cognitive flexibility, an equally significant part being resilient and ready to bounce back in difficulties, appears to be partially determined by sufficient sleep. Cognitive flexibility usually means you're able to view different points of view and alter your thinking in reaction to new data and scenarios. For instance, if you are angry that your spouse had been getting home late, you may change your opinion when you understand that he was changing a bike to get a buddy. However, when you're sleep-deprived, you might remain stuck being mad that he/she is overdue and become slow to modify your response based on additional facts. This difficulty in adapting your thinking to new info is likely to make it easier to become overwhelmed by your feelings.

Whenever you don't have sufficient sleep, you lose your eligibility to self-assess--to ascertain if something you are doing is helping resolve an issue or making it more challenging. It is also more difficult to understand somebody else's view. For instance, you might be unsympathetic to a teenage son's perception that his life is going to be destroyed if he starts to school. These issues can raise the disagreements that you have with the ones you love.

Enhancing Your Sleep

Preventing your sleep difficulties will not be simple, but it is going to probably have positive results on both the emotional and your bodily wellness. Just like most issues, the answers to sleep problems aren't instant but need slow implementation, together with the results becoming more obvious with time. The significant improvements you will get in your ability to deal with your feelings would probably be well worth your efforts.

CREATE A COMFORTABLE SLEEP ENVIRONMENT

Your environment might impact your sleep more than you imagine. These tips can help you make your bedroom a relaxing escape so that with the time, you will anticipate being on your bed instead of stressing it since the location in which you toss and turn each evening. The very best environment for sleeping is dependent upon your tastes.

Your bedroom might be more relaxing and conducive to sleeping if it is decorated in a manner that doesn't disturb you. Additionally, an area that is organized and lovely is very likely to feel much more relaxing than a cluttered one. You will probably want a serene environment, one who feels secure.

The images, the artwork, the novels --all of the items in the area should be mentally neutral or have a link to something favorable. Eliminate anything that disturbs you, which makes you feel stressed, or even has a link to something damaging --like a mattress that belonged to some disliked relative.

If you can, decorate your bedroom just as a no-stress zone. Avoid doing some activities in your bedroom, which may bring tension inside that area, such as work-related or work pursuits. As soon as you start using your bedroom just for sleeping and resting, your mind and body will come to see that the bedroom is a place to unwind.

Being physically comfortable is likewise significant for a great night's sleep. Just as the budget will permit, put money into a mattress and cushions that fit your preferences. Test different mattresses at a shop to determine what seems better for you. Many men and women sleep well in a darkened room.

If you can't keep light from penetrating your bedroom at night, then try out a sleep mask. You will also sleep much better if the temperature is more best suited to you. A fantastic night temperature for most individuals is between 65 and 72 degrees Fahrenheit. If your feet tend to become cold, perhaps sleep in jeans. Some people today sleep well with silent, and many others are sleeping more intensely with background sound, like a radio or T.V. in a minimal volume. Experiment with quiet, silent voices, and relaxing music to learn what works great. You may try playing audiobooks, records of white sound or records of rain, sea waves, or other nature seems that will help you unwind. Or maybe you like to use earplugs.

EVENING ACTIVITIES AND ROUTINES

Engaging in relaxing and easing actions for the hour or two before going to bed will help you become prepared for sleeping. If you generally exercise in the day, then try exercising before. Although exercise can cause you to feel exhausted, it is difficult to really fall asleep in a couple of hours after physical activity. Watching scary pictures or bothering programs, finishing work-related or work activities, and considering your issues may make it more difficult to fall asleep. The information can cause emotions that hinder relaxing and multitasking.

The light from computer or television screens might help keep you awake more also, even when you have turned them off. Rather, consider reading a novel or mild magazine, or listening to soothing music, doing puzzles, or even speaking with relatives. Dimming the lights an hour or so before you retire, wearing loose, comfy clothes allows you to prepare for the remainder. If a bath or a tub will calm you, then it could be a part of your bedtime routine. If not, perform night hygiene, like washing your face along with brushing your teeth, half an hour or so before bedtime. It can be valuable to do identical relaxing activities daily.

Your body will become used to your routine, with the consequence which you will feel tired after performing your daily activities. Moving to sleep and getting up at precisely the same time every day can also be valuable for the same reason.

CALMING EMOTIONS AND THOUGHTS

Enrolling in bed not being able to sleep may be an unpleasant encounter. Perhaps you get angry considering how tired you're going to be in the daytime. Perhaps you've got an especially demanding day beforehand, and you also worry you will not have the ability to execute the best you can. Perhaps you consider just how much you really hate not sleeping.

While natural and understandable, those ideas and anxieties make getting to sleep much more difficult. Accepting that you are not sleeping is a significant step in reducing your distress and stress, which makes it increasingly difficult to sleep soundly. Perhaps you can alter the idea that you despise the fact of being unable to sleep, and now you wish that was not correct. You could still break. Consider releasing muscle tension, too.

Progressive muscle relaxation, as an instance, reduces stress and helps the body unwind. Maybe all of your concerns come flooding in your mind as you lie down to sleep soundly. If you are emotionally stimulated or cannot quit considering issues, then attempt scaling. Then occupy your head with a job such as counting backward in a hundred from threes or considering a different zoo animal for every letter of the alphabet. Do the job.

If you find that if you are in bed, your ideas race or are considering concerns, things you have to do, or suggestions to add action, consider keeping a pencil and paper to the bed, so you can write down whatever is in your mind. At times it's useful to write down a specific time when you're concentrating on what is about you. For instance, intend to provide that difficulty you are consumed along with your entire focus at 10:00 a.m. the following moment. This straightforward action frequently works well to allow you to forego repetitive thoughts. You might feel an instantaneous relief and soon fall asleep.

A guided-imagery recording might help you concentrate your attention on some relaxing or pleasant experience rather than the anxieties or issues looping on the mind. Adhering to a voice directing you to envision walking across a beautiful shore may function better than simply imagining yourself. Possessing a friend or somebody who you like recording a guided-imagery workout for you might be much more successful.

LIMIT CAFFEINE AND ALCOHOL

For many individuals, drinking alcohol or caffeine after a specific period makes it difficult to lose excess weight to remain asleep during the nighttime, or even both. Some men and women who drink alcohol or caffeine don't have any difficulty falling asleep but frequently wake up early and cannot return to sleep. If you are among those whose difficulty is not falling asleep but remaining asleep, you might not see the impact that alcohol and caffeine have on the human body and your sleeping --even once you consume them nicely before bedtime.

If you were able to use a much better night's sleep, then consider decreasing the total amount of caffeine and alcohol you have for a week and then see what happens.

ADDRESS MEDICAL CONCERNS

Speak with your doctor about the sleeping issues you are having. She might consult with a professional, who will evaluate you for sleeping disorders like sleep apnea, a frequent disorder where you breathe properly or irregularly as you are sleeping. Sleep apnea does interrupt your rest; it may cause serious health problems and is associated with depression. Consult your doctor if any medications you are taking might interfere with your sleeping, as several antidepressants have been known to do so.

Your physician may alter the medicine, or maybe he/she can make you take such drugs in the morning rather than at night. Your healthcare provider may also talk about different alternatives with you personally, like maybe including a prescription sleeping medicine. Over-the-counter sleep aids could also be useful. Supplements of nitric oxide, a hormone that can help restrain your adrenal cycles, are usually considered safe if used in reduced doses. The supplement could have side effects, like reduced body weight, morning grogginess, little alterations in blood pressure, along with vivid fantasies. All these side effects disappear if you stop taking the nutritional supplement.

MAKE A PLAN AND KEEP A SLEEP DIARY

A sleep diary is a list of your waking and sleeping times, together with related data, like actions you can do before bed and just how much caffeine you consume every day. Keeping a sleep diary for many months will help you identify methods to boost your sleep. When you start to keep a sleep journal, do not create any changes in your sleep regimen. Have a week just to collect information regarding your existing habits.

Document the number of hours that you slept every night and the time you went to bed along with the time you woke up. Then write down what changes you will make for your bedroom, your actions, and patterns before bedtime, along with your alcohol and caffeine consumption (see tips above). Decide how you are going to tackle any health issues you've got and the way you are going to manage disruptive thoughts and emotions.

Be specific. The instance sleep journal below may function as a guide in creating your sleep program. As soon as you've established a sleeping program, follow along for four months. Keep a sleep diary for every one of those four months. You can add any other actions you know are essential to monitor, like if you chose a tub or restricted your tv or computer time before going to sleep every evening.

The more carefully you follow your strategy, the more likely you will find the desired outcomes. In the base of each column, listing the number of hours of sleep you need to have and how relaxed you feel as if you awaken the following day, with 0 being the smallest relaxed you have ever believed. Five will be very relaxed; you have ever believed in the afternoon.

	Example	Monday	Tuesday	Wednesday	Thursday	Friday	Saturday	Sunday
Set Bedtime Routine	Completed							
Set Bed and Wake – up Times	Yes							
Early Exercise	Yes							
Light Dinner	Salad with Chicken							
Caffeine	2 Coffees							
Alcohol	One glass wine at 6							

	Example	Monday	Tuesday	Wednesday	Thursday	Friday	Saturday	Sunday
Soothing Activity Before Bed	Reading							
Calm Emotions	Guided Imagery							
Dark Room	Yes							
Comfortable Temperature	Yes							
Keep your mind bust with a boring task	Did not need							
Visualization	Yes							
Write Your	Yes							

	Exam ple	Mon day	Tues day	Wedne sday	Thur sday	Fri day	Satur day	Sun day
Though ts								
Noise/Q uiet	White noise							
Accepta nce	Yes							
Hour Slept	8							
Restful ness on waking 0-5	4							

After four weeks, then assess your results. Can you raise or boost your sleeping in any way? Perhaps you discovered feeling rested, using more energy throughout the daytime, not stirring in the morning, falling asleep easily, or not having an early day slump. Four weeks is not a sufficient amount of time to practice a brand new sleep regimen, so if you notice favorable modifications but are not yet getting adequate sleep, then maintain filling out your sleep journal for the following two weeks. If you still are not getting sufficient sleep, speak to your physician.

Exercise

Exercise is just one of the very best strategies to keep extreme feelings in check. Being physically active will help regulate your mood as good as or better than drugs, for these reasons:

- It functions as a diversion from things that are bothering you.
- It reduces muscular strain.
- It raises and balances dopamine and norepinephrine (significant neurotransmitters involved in the mood).
- It enhances endurance by demonstrating that you're able to succeed in controlling your own emotions.
- It may break the encounter of becoming helpless and trapped.

Along with helping to regulate your mood, exercise improves your capacity to understand. It enhances your focus and capability to accommodate and bounce back after an error. When you are practicing new coping skills, just how nicely you process new info and recuperate from choices that don't work is obviously significant. Exercise also boosts cognitive flexibility.

As mentioned previously, cognitive flexibility is the ability to incorporate new information in your comprehension of a circumstance. The same ability also entails employing new problem-solving approaches and utilizing information in creative ways. Being physically active helps alleviate and fix the consequences of pressure in the entire human body.

When you are stressed, your body creates cortisol. This hormone puts you back on a very high alert and mobilizes the body's resources to assist you in reacting to immediate bodily dangers. Although a lot of our anxiety results from emotional dangers, psychological threats, and anxieties about the long run, our bodies react only as if the danger were immediate and physical. If the danger is a real physiological individual, you can reduce your cortisol by choosing an unusual physical activity, like fighting or escaping.

If the danger is emotional, psychological, or fanciful, on the flip side, there is generally no such actions you may take, and thus your cortisol level stays high. Because of this, it is difficult to think clearly, as your system is primed for actions, not logical thought-- that the trend is to determine prospective dangers everywhere.

If you are under continuous anxiety, overexposure to cortisol and other stress hormones may also disrupt the body's function and contribute to cardiovascular disease, stress, depression, weight gain, sleep issues, and memory impairment. Exercise can be very powerful in assisting you to handle overwhelming feelings. Some people today notice lower stress levels following six months of cardio workout. Also, as your capacity to focus and understand, your physical health will improve. You might also have fun if you opt for an activity you like. Additionally, other attempts to boost your ability to deal with your emotions; it will work nicely if you exercise frequently. Identify which sort of activity may work best is vital since you are more inclined to start and keep a task that fulfills your tastes and lifestyle.

Your Exercise Style

The next questions are intended to assist you to consider more specifically about actions you would be likely to perform. Write your own answers.

Are you comfortable exercising on your own or with friends?

_____

_____

Do you like competition?

_____

_____

Would you wish to set actions, like attending to a dance class, or would you need variety? Are there any activities you would like to understand, like boxing or even rock climbing?

_____

_____

Are you more inclined to exercise first thing in the afternoon or in the early day?

_____

_____

Would you like to integrate exercise into your everyday routine, not utilize specific equipment or scheduled occasions?

_____

_____

DOING IT ALONE

If you choose to work out alone, look at making your routine. Write down two or three lists of exercises which can take you approximately half an hour, and perform them five days weekly. They may consist of jumping jacks, toe touches, marching in place, jumping rope, or hula hooping. Fitness magazines, publications, and movies frequently have workout routines that you could follow if you do not wish to make your own. Yoga movies are a fantastic alternative too. Or biking, walking all around your area, at a playground, or even on a college campus might attract you.

HARNESS YOUR COMPETITIVE SPIRIT

If you are inspired by rivalry, you may want to join a club or group like racquetball, bowling, or even golfing. Perhaps you'd like to challenge a buddy to ninety times of workout and determine if you can finish the exercises that you select collectively. You may establish a contest with yourself: Would you exercise more or walk a bit farther than you did a week?

JUST PART OF YOUR DAY

If you would like to incorporate exercise into your everyday routine, then there are lots of strategies to achieve that. After you walk to confirm the email, then go back and forth a couple of times. Park far away from the entry of the destination and walk quickly out of your vehicle to the doorway. Just take the stairs rather than an elevator. Lift your supermarket bags up and down as you take them to a vehicle. If you watch T.V., do leg lifts and other exercises.

MAKE A PLAN AND FOLLOW IT

It is time to get going. What exactly are you really going to do? The more specific you are, the more probable it is that you'll follow along with the action. Stating that you will "visit the gym now at 9:00 a.m. and walk to the treadmill for about fifteen minutes" is far better than saying you are likely to "begin exercising."

Carry this program along with you--may be utilizing a monitoring application on your smartphone to quantify your progress employing it. Or maybe you place your strategy on your fridge so you could remind yourself to stay to it and graph your progress. Assessing your new behavior can allow you to follow along developing a fresh new habit.

	Exercise	Time Spent
Monday		
Tuesday		
Wednesday		
Thursday		
Friday		
Saturday		
Sunday		

Find a means to keep yourself inspired. Imagine how much your exercise level increases in 3 months. Reward yourself for every week you follow your strategy. Give yourself a deal, like a cup of your favorite tea or viewing an episode of your favorite T.V. series, once you exercise. If you get discouraged, keep in mind that beginning any new habit can be difficult. When you begin exercising, you might notice just how out of shape you're. In reality, you might have been preventing exercise partially to avoid to face that fact.

Being a newcomer at any action is humbling and, at times, embarrassing. Additionally, if you first begin working out, being physically active does not feel great: your muscles may ache, and you're going to wish you're relaxing on your sofa. There are many reasons and explanations you may list not to exercise. Just bear in mind the benefits you will gain by frequently exercising, even if you merely walk around the block or lift a bottle of detergent a number of times with each hand. It is possible to do it!

Structuring Your Time

Emotionally sensitive individuals frequently say that using construction in their daily life, for example, scheduled times to perform specific actions, helps them achieve tasks. That is partly because a dedication to do anything at a specific period is more difficult to dismiss than a vague "I will do it shortly."

Accomplishing an essential job generally is mentally satisfying (or alleviating) and makes it possible to prevent the anxiety that results in waiting until the final minute. Whenever you have appointments classes to attend, actions to do, and individuals to meet, you are less likely to be centered on your own emotions. Because of this, those feelings will not seem so extreme and might pass more readily.

You might be the type of person who participates when you have planned every hour of your daily life, or you might be the type of person who seems overwhelmed with detailed preparation. Additionally, you might have an inclination to underestimate or overestimate how much time it is going to require you to do things and just how much you're able to perform daily. Possibly the constraints and stress of a tight program boost your anxiety over their help.

When you attempt to perform more than you've got time for, you might find you do not have enough time to perform necessary tasks. On the flip side, having too small to do may bring you to lethargy, despair, or even the belief you haven't anything to contribute. For each of these reasons, locating the ideal quantity of construction will need trial and error.

Find the Right Amount of Structure

Establish a comprehensive program, one which comprises many daily tasks both in the home and outside your house. Consider ᵢₒₙₑ ing that program weekly. Then establish another schedule that has only a couple of things to do every day. Utilize that program weekly.

If you do not work outside the home, your initial schedule may look like that:

9:00 Wake up, eat breakfast, a test program

10:00 Exercise

11:00 Shower and apparel 11:30 Needed actions (store for the grocery store, clean the house, pay bills, etc.)

1:30 Lunch

2:00 Volunteer, apply for jobs, research for college, read

3:00 Creative action (compose, paint, create jewelry, cook, and work in the backyard)

4:00 Contact buddies, see neighbors, call your family

6:00 Dinner

Your next program might have put times for a couple of jobs or merely a brief list of what you will do, without any specified instances.

When you have followed every kind of program for a week, then evaluate your expertise. Which kind of program worked?

Observing a program might be hard, yet it is going to assist you in making decisions regarding time obligations. If you discovered you're too active, then you might have to drop a few actions. On the flip side, maybe you discovered you wanted more in your program.

Paying Attention for Your Staff

Emotionally sensitive men and women tend to be especially reactive to their environment. You might not be familiar in crowds or might despise small, enclosed spaces. A messy or cluttered area can cause you to feel irritable, raise your negative thoughts about yourself, also lead to overpowering feelings. Let us say you can find dirty dishes piled on your kitchen sink, drain glasses left hanging about your living space, and newspapers and publications all over the floor.

Clothes are strewn all over the furniture in the bedroom. What message does that send to you personally? What emotions are you really going to encounter in this kind of setting? If a cluttered room disturbs you, maybe one reason is that for you personally, the jumble reflects a scarcity of self-value. The other possibility is that the condition of your house informs you that you are out of control or cannot handle your life. Perhaps the clutter in your home reflects an awareness of apathy or powerlessness.

For one of these reasons, meeting a mess in your house daily can help determine how you think about yourself. Additionally, a cluttered house may enhance your isolation, even if you will not invite folks over whenever your property is in disarray. Wait a moment; you may be thinking. My home is a wreck since I have been gloomy, depressed, fearful, or helpless.

My home is a wreck because I believe I am powerless. My home is a wreck because I am emotionally sensitive, and handling my feelings takes all of my energy. This could possibly be true. The issue is that using a cluttered or muddy residence may increase a down disposition, absence of self-respect, ideas of helplessness, ideas of being overrun, and migraines. And, as in most conditions, the issue stinks. If your property is cluttered, you might be committing yourself the concept that "cluttered" behavior is fine. Imagine you are sitting in your living room watching a film on T.V., eating the last of your ice cream in the carton, and enjoying popcorn.

There are newspapers everywhere, empty soda cans and candy wrappers on the ground, and outstanding bills sprinkled on the coffee table. After the film is finished, it is late, and you are feeling lethargic by junk foods.

What are the odds you'll set your spoon in your dishwasher, throw off the ice cream carton, and place the rice away popcorn? What are the opportunities you will cover the bills? If your home was neat and clean, the odds are higher you would tidy up after yourself and pay off the invoices. Even if you did not do this night, you would be likely to perform it the next moment.

Look at making little changes that can make your house pleasant and purposeful. You may want to wash for ten minutes every day in one room. Perhaps start with the bedroom, in which you wake up daily. Perhaps you can clean for ten minutes each afternoon and ten minutes during the night. A different approach is to perform one job every day. For instance, on Monday, you clean a load of clothing. On Tuesday you clean dishes. If you have too many possessions, then look at sorting them out. Maintain the things which matter for you personally and give away the rest. Maintain the program possible and manageable. Track your progress. Reward yourself for every step you take.

Putting It All Together

In my experience, caring for your physical well-being, structuring your own time, and coordinating your surroundings are among the most important measures people can do to control their feelings and make a feeling of well-being. However, focusing on getting more excellent sleeping, getting more exercise, and becoming more organized is somewhat difficult, and you might doubt the significance of accomplishing such things. If you are thinking, certainly there is some new treatment or medicine which can make more of a difference. I recommend you to run an experiment: place the changes dealt with in this chapter into position, and assess for yourself the differences they make in your life.

Chapter #4
Mindfulness

Mindfulness, part of several psychological treatments, is a straightforward concept to comprehend, although not simple to put into practice.

Meditation as "paying attention in a specific way: on purpose, at the current instant, and nonjudgmentally." It usually means keeping your head in the here and now. For instance, if you are eating dinner with your husband, then the focus is on your spouse; even if that is where you desire the focus to become (that is the "on purpose" portion of this definition).

You are also focusing solely on what it is possible to see, without translating or judging. To keep the example, you may observe that your spouse is grinning as he speaks. That might be monitoring. Believing that he is a jerk is a decision. Having the ability to concentrate your attention on exactly what you see is a wonderful ability that may greatly influence your feeling of well-being.

As soon as you start working on maintaining your ideas about the here, you'll be calmer and less worried. Nevertheless, people generally are not inherently mindful. Our ideas have a tendency to leap from one subject to another, frequently in an unfocused manner.

Our minds frequently wander in the past, ruminating over damaging events we're powerless to alter; or to the future, stressing over unfavorable events that have not even occurred. If you are emotionally sensitive, then your ideas and extreme feelings may frequently make it particularly difficult to be "at present."

You are more inclined to be bashful and on the protector, hyper-alert to potential psychological threats. Training your brain to concentrate on the here will require exercise, but the outcomes will be well worth the attempt. You may be aware both of everything is out of you, such as individuals, things, or noises, and your inner experience-- your ideas, senses, and feelings.

Mindfulness of your inner experience can allow you to step back out of your emotions as opposed to being engulfed by them simply. It is going to provide you with a pause between your feelings and ideas while you reactivate, so that you'll be able to make thoughtful conclusions. Whenever you're aware, you will not get lost in concerns about the long run or despair in advance.

You are going to accept others and yourself. Your emotions will not have the ability to take control. Regardless of the benefits of being aware of your inner experience, you could be reluctant to be aware of your feelings, especially the painful ones. However, being aware of your feelings is an increasingly essential ability.

Mindfulness of Emotions

It's simple to feel that the existence of difficult emotions, such as sadness and harm, means you have done something wrong. It could appear that different men and women are happy most of the time, and if they've problems, they solve them quickly and easily. A character in a TV series, as an instance, might appear able to solve just about any dilemma at the close of the event.

Popular novels and films also perpetuate the myth of the happy ending, even if characters confront with overwhelming difficulties. Commercials could have you feel you can be pleased if you drive the ideal vehicle or utilize the ideal deodorant. Individuals in your life might appear to believe you may be much better off if only you would follow their easy guidance --for instance, to receive work, to find a backbone, or even to stop being upset. These impacts can lead one to believe that others may easily conquer the type of issues you always fight with, which means that you're less competent than they are.

If you are emotionally sensitive, then you might already fear the extreme strain of difficult emotions. Along with the concept that feeling lonely or sad causes you to feel not ordinary, a loser, as well as "mad" simply adds to hesitation to encounter any emotions aside from agreeable ones. Everybody is unhappy, lonely, upset, and hurt sometimes. Real-life issues are often not simple to resolve, and it might need quite a very long time to get things to change. Comparing yourself to other people who you believe having it better than you in pursuing material merchandise to make yourself feel much better generally creates more distress.

If Only---Then I Would Be Happy

You might imagine that joy is caused by attaining targets and attaining possessions. You might believe You'll be happy Once You have more cash, when you get this promotion, or whenever you're a parent. Or you can believe, If I can only find a person to enjoy, then I will understand happiness.

The issue is that if you visit the long term to get enjoyment, you cannot be at peace currently. Even once you obtain exactly what you wish for, then there is always something more to get. You might believe someone to be very happy; you have to think and act as the others do. Therefore, you look to other people on how improve in living your life. If you're able to do exactly what they do, then you believe you will be glad and live your life the "appropriate" way.

This typically results in comparisons to other people --typically people that you think do better than you. Maybe you compare career-wise to somebody near the very top of your career or the very prosperous individual that you understand. You may compare your physical fitness level to that of a colleague that works out every day. Assessing the very best attributes of the others is very likely to maximize your discontent. Getting mindful involves residing in the present time rather than stressing yourself, your emotions, your feelings, or alternative men and women. Practicing mindfulness can allow you to halt the distress that comes from comparing yourself to people you think are happier than you and estimating your psychological encounter.

Finding a Balance

Occasionally, your ideas could be negative. As an instance, perhaps it appears that life is just one big battle, although others' lifestyles are a ride. This enables you to feel unhappy and resentful. Or maybe you concentrate on just one way you may wind up being happy, like getting into a specific college or getting married at a particular date. This may result in feeling despair if you cannot do these items. Believing that joy is an either/or proposal --you're happy, or you are not--is similar to painting the complicated and diverse image of your life in just one color.

It may direct you to get caught up in negativity if every portion of your life is more difficult; you might become angry, focusing just on the difficulties. For instance, if a person talks to you rudely in the airport, then you will find it impossible to delight in the initial hours of your holiday.

Getting alert to the complete truth of scenarios you are experiencing can allow you to balance your own emotions, to avoid to suffer needlessly. If you generally concentrate on or become conscious only of difficulties, focus on recalling the positive sides. List the pros and cons of a circumstance, and consider them in terms of their real significance. Then concentrate on the particulars of the favorable experiences. Provide your undivided attention to reviewing these advantages on multiple occasions.

This procedure will to help you find the whole instead of over-focusing on the downside. You probably have either/or expectations in expecting events too. Imagine you get an invitation to lunch by a friend you have not seen in a little while. You cannot wait to see him. The day you are supposed to meet with him, you are feeling excited. You then recall that the last time you met for supper that he informed you how well his occupation was about and on the new house he purchased.

You subsequently judged yourself rather than performing too. You recall this repeatedly occurs if you find this buddy. Now, rather than being eager to see your buddy, you wish you had not consented to meet with him. You move from seeing just the favorable to experiencing just the negative. Becoming mindful of all of the elements of your relationships can allow you to balance your own emotions. In the example mentioned above, the consciousness of your enthusiasm to realize your pal and your inclination to compare him can help you remain balanced. Becoming mindful of the entire image before you visit him will allow you to prepare yourself by letting go of your self-judgments. If you're able to not just be conscious of the optimistic once you're angry, but also aware of the positive aspects of a scenario when you are feeling a strong positive emotion, then you can reduce your mental ups and downs.

Becoming Aware of More than One Emotion

Becoming mindful of all of the emotions you are experiencing, paying attention to all those feelings which are not as extreme in addition to those which are more extreme. Although one emotion might appear to dominate at any time, we frequently encounter many different feelings simultaneously.

For instance, you might be pleased about finding a new job in a different state. However, you are sad because it means moving and leaving great buddies. You might also be a little afraid of the struggle waiting ahead, also, to hurt somebody by stating you're bragging about your great luck. If you concentrate on just one of these feelings, you will eliminate information and psychological balance.

If you are conscious of a single emotion, then ask yourself what's there--search for different emotions which may also exist.

Develop a Pause

Thinking before you act demands that you just pause to discover your ideas and feelings and determine what you will say and do.

Maybe that sounds impossible as you have experienced you emotions in your own emotions for ages. Nevertheless, through mindfulness, you are able to practice being conscious of your inner experience, so you're ready to detect it without being fully caught up inside.

You will have the ability to say, "That is wrath," or "That hurt," without acting on these feelings. Consider how frequently you repent of actions you chose if you're emotional, and just how much it may be helpful if you can do this just a bit less frequently.

With mindfulness, if you encounter an emotional storm instead of getting swept off your toes or charging forward freely throughout the pouring rain, then you can detect the storm and wait patiently until your mind becomes clear again so you can think before acting. If you practice awareness of your mental experience and celebrating and accepting the truth as it is, without interpretation or judgment, your emotions will be moderated, and you are able to handle them effectively. The advantages are many. Yet beginning and keeping a mindfulness practice can be an issue.

Practicing Mindfulness

You do not have to meditate to practice mindfulness. Typically, the perfect method to begin practicing mindfulness is be more mindful of actions and objects.

Mindfulness of objects

Becoming mindful of things entails concentrating your attention on something out of yourself. You may practice this at any given moment since there are always things around to concentrate. You may try the next exercise in time if you are feeling overwhelmed by your ideas or feelings.

Mindfulness of Everyday objects

Opt for any item in the area --it does not matter what it's. For three minutes, concentrate solely on this particular thing. Really watch it. For instance, if you are conscious of a pencil, then you may detect its feel and ridges, its own contour, how sharp or worn it is, its colors, how it feels in your hand, and just how thick it is.

You will observe that your ideas jump around to several other items if you are attempting to keep your focus on the item. You might consider your kids, filing your taxes, the job project that must be performed, your buddy who is ill, and the guests arriving for dinner elsewhere. This lack of attention can be excruciating. You might believe you are not performing the practice properly. Suffering from distractions can be a standard portion of mindfulness, nevertheless. If you are frequently diverted, it does not imply mindfulness won't operate, or you cannot get it done correctly. If you become conscious of a diversion, admit it gently and bring your attention back to this item within the room. Initially, you might find it beneficial to have a fixed period or action to practice mindfulness. You may practice mindfulness while performing simple, everyday pursuits. You might opt to be aware when you wake up, possibly by focusing on your residence's first morning sounds.

You can practice mindfulness when brushing your teeth by focusing solely on brushing your teeth, on feeling the toothpaste in your mouth, and the feeling of this brush bristling onto your teeth. Watch what is important to consider brushing your teeth without stress. You may observe that you evaluate your look as you appear from the mirror, or you may believe being conscious of cleaning your teeth is absurd.

As soon as you end up noticing your attention drifting, gently bring your attention back to anything you are doing. At times, despite the fact that you're practicing mindfulness, you will observe an emotion originating. Do not dismiss the emotion, but do not allow it to take over your focus.

Rather, attempt to gently be conscious of the emotion as part of your own experience. Title the emotion. Say to yourself, for instance, "I've sadness." Sometimes, just recognizing that the emotion in this manner can help loosen its grasp on your focus. On the flip side, you may opt to be more conscious of despair, especially if you have not been conscious of being gloomy. You may notice where precisely you believe it within your own body and what ideas you've got.

You may know about what's triggered the despair. On the flip side, if you are well aware of your despair, understand the reason behind this and have invested some time expressing it, then you may be better served by recognizing the emotion, then gently bringing your attention back to anything you are doing (e.g., cleaning your teeth). To remain aware of action if emotions are distracting you, then try breathing deeply and naming the emotion, as indicated previously.

If the emotion doesn't have any significance to the current instant, you might choose to point out that to yourself. For instance, if you are unhappy about something which occurred previously, you may say to yourself, "That was miserable. But that was then, and now is now." If you are concerned about the future in some manner, you may say to yourself, "That is a frightening idea, but that idea is not true today." Imagine the emotion and draw your attention back to the current moment. You might want to do this differently.

Practice mindfulness daily, irrespective of how your day is going or what emotions you are experiencing. If it appears that the evening is too busy to practice mindfulness, that is the ideal day to the clinic. You may be cautious even if you're in a rush. If you proceed fast but mindfully, you will probably be more able in whatever you are doing, since you'll be distracted. Keeping an eye on your mindfulness exercise can allow you to make it part of your routine. Having mindfulness become part of your everyday tasks --for instance, which makes it a custom to become aware whenever you are driving--is still a fantastic means to incorporate mindfulness in your life.

Assessing Your Mindfulness Practice

Keep tabs on your mindfulness exercise for a single week. Write everything you did mindfully in the following areas (or in a diary or laptop) every day.

Day 1: _____

Day 2: _____

Day 3: _____

Day 4: _____

Day 5: _____

Day 6: _____

Day 7: _____

Now describe your own experience. What did you find about becoming mindful?

_____

_____

_____

Consider the way you're able to incorporate mindfulness further into your ordinary life. Maybe you'll continue to be more mindful in a specific time of day or even performing a specific activity. Write down your thoughts.

_____

_____

_____

Mindfulness of Emotions and Thoughts

Strong feelings scream for your attention, which explains precisely why pushing them off does not function in the very long term. If you push your own emotions from your consciousness since you don't wish to cope with what triggered them, that they might return after a while, triggered by something different. For instance, perhaps an incident in the office makes you mad at your boss. However, you also do not admit your anger as you are fearful of being dismissed. When you are at home, you shout at your kid for not selecting his clothing. You might be disappointed about your kid's cluttered room, but the most crucial reason for your anger was the episode on the job.

When you are conscious of your emotions, then you can observe the sense and let it pass. Becoming mindful of emotions can initially raise their strength, which may be embarrassing, so start by being aware of emotions that are not too difficult to control. To begin with, see the sensation. The emotion will construct, and you might fear that if you continue to give it your focus, it will not relent. But if you turn off the emotion whenever it's building, then you won't understand through experience, the emotion will eventually peak and then dissipate by itself.

So stick with the emotion, simply notice this, permit it to pass. Remind yourself that it is only an emotion. Emotions last just a brief period if you don't push them away or build them up. When you are aware of how you are feeling, the emotion which has been screaming to your focus will probably feel heard and will then be silent. Becoming aware of your feelings can be difficult to perform all on your own. You might desire to find support from a therapist to understand mindfulness of your own emotions. Not all therapists are trained in mindfulness methods, so make sure you ask first.

WORRY THOUGHTS AND ANXIETY

Many mentally sensitive men and women are worried. Worrying may appear to assist you to stay away from unfortunate occasions or keep you from being caught off guard. Maybe you think about the habit of stressing the price that you pay to get ready for adverse events. Even though the events people fear do occasionally occur, we really do not understand what the future could deliver. Stress and anxiety for the future are so ineffective.

To put it differently, they are not really worth their psychological price. Additionally, if you stress, your brain is not in the current instant. You are less able to concentrate on what is happening today, as you are busy thinking about events that have not happened. Rather than stressing, practice being aware of your ideas, accepting that you have anxieties, and bringing back your mind into the current without stressing. With time, you might discover you could remain in the current or bring back into the current more readily and reduce your stressful thoughts.

MINDFULNESS AND THE WISH TO CONTROL

Mentally sensitive men and women, specifically, frequently want to control what happens within their own lives as a means to prevent being hurt. Maybe you want, build, and organize your times in minute detail in a bid to make life predictable. Perhaps you rehearse what you will say in discussions. Maybe you elicit claims from other people as a means of attempting to get control. Perhaps you ask a lot of questions to be sure that people are not angry with you or they're not likely to fall their connection with you.

Overcoming your fears and be aware of what disturbs you--like change, doubt, and the feelings that include these experiences--could be challenging. Being mindful of your anxieties and efforts in controlling everything will be useful in getting rid of behaviors that are not effective methods of coping with your feelings in the very long run.

Identifying Your Efforts to Control What You Can't Control

As you proceed throughout the day, notice whenever you encounter a feeling of thoughts or anxiety that you need something in a particular way. On a piece of newspaper (e.g., in a diary or laptop), listing the following information:

- The Circumstance
- Your Level of stress
- Your ideas about the circumstance
- What you are attempting to restrain

Repeat this action three times. Whenever you have done this for three days, consider the scenarios you composed. Watch what patterns you'll be able to identify. Do you typically feel apprehensive about whether a person would like you or become mad at you? Have you got a pattern of trying to restrain the feelings or ideas that others have around you personally?

Maybe you typically try to restrain the emotions or choices of somebody who you adore. Later on, attempt to approach those scenarios in a careful manner. Mindfulness involves the approval of everything you encounter, such as uncomfortable feelings.

Maintaining your emotions includes not behaving in ineffective techniques to decrease these feelings. Mindfulness is an antidote to both prevention and attempts to restrain. Any time, you practice mindfulness; then you are working on your own capability to accept the uncertainty and change and this can diminish your psychological suffering.

Wait

Whenever you are angry and have an impulse to act in your emotions, then the next measures can help you choose the best plan of action. See the emotion. Step back and watch your experience of this emotion. Be cautious of the way the emotion feels on your own body, what triggered the emotion, so your own ideas about the emotion or the circumstance, and some other urges you've got.

The emotion can ebb and flow, becoming stronger until it slowly decreases in power. Accept that you are with emotion, maybe you do not need to control it. Acceptance means allowing the emotion to occur while recognizing that you don't need to act on it. Although sometimes you might feel controlled by your emotions, you do not need to worry. Frequently no activity is essential.

If you are emotionally sensitive, then it is very likely you experience an impulse to do something which will help you get rid of this emotion. Whatever it might be, this activity may have turned into a routine in your life.

For instance, maybe you repeatedly look for reassurance from other people that they care for you as a means of attempting to ward off despair or fear of reduction. Acceptance means allowing the emotion to occur while recognizing that you don't need to act on it or from its efforts to control your feelings by simply resisting or trying to eliminate it. These are only another method of letting your emotions control you, as you are still allowing them to dictate your behavior. Rather, be aware that it's fine to feel whatever you are feeling. Investigate the info the emotion provides you. If you are mad about a job, maybe your anger will be telling you it is time to search a new occupation. Looking for the advice your emotions supply can result in effective actions that can allow you to proceed in your life. Take some time. Know that the emotion will soon pass. Permit it. If you can, do not take any actions until you are calmer, so that you're able to think through your activities more clearly.

Practicing WAIT

Exercise WAIT (Watch, Accept, Investigate, Take some time) and answer these questions regarding your own experience.

See the emotion: What do you see about your own experience?

_____

_____

Recall the emotion: What's it like to take the emotion? Can you have urges to halt the emotion in some manner?

_____

_____

Inquire into the emotion: What advice did your emotion provide you?

_____

_____

Take some time: How are your ideas about what actions to choose different following the emotion?

_____

_____

Know and Trust Your Internal Experience

Mindfulness of your inner experience (feelings and thoughts specifically) will permit you to understand what you are feeling and not to act in your own emotions impulsively. When you are in a position to tag and handle your emotions efficiently and think sensibly, you will learn how to trust your ideas, your choices, and also your psychological experience.

95

You will get a better awareness of your own identity. Many mentally sensitive men and women find they have problems with infectious emotions: they "grab" others' feelings. Any moment you're with somebody who's angry, you might become angry too. After the emotion calms, you could be perplexed by the way you felt, since it did not actually match exactly with what was occurring to you.

Mindfulness will provide you with the chance to pause, so it is possible to identify what portion of your psychological encounter, if any, isn't your own. Pause, and also be cautious --regardless of what emotions you are having. If you understand you are angry because somebody else was angry, then this information can allow you to deal with your feelings. Mindfulness of feelings is a very first step in correctly identifying your inner experience, which can assist you to trust yourself rather than relying on other people to tag your feelings and exactly what ideas you should have. Finally, your associations will probably be rocky, since you will not be quite as fearful of folks leaving you. You will have much more calmness, self-acceptance, along with self-compassion.

Everyday Mindfulness

Assessing mindfulness of your feelings on a daily basis can allow you to learn to become more mindful more mechanically. If you are emotionally sensitive, then no doubt, you will have many chances on any particular evening to practice mindfulness of your own emotions.

Mindfulness in Relationships

One example of using mindfulness on a daily basis is being aware of the answers of other people. Imagine your spouse comes home with no item you requested him to pick up in the shop. You get mad. You do not give him an opportunity to clarify, as you don't wish to listen to some lame explanation. You know why: He must think that you are not important enough to recall what you asked. Nevertheless, your premise could be incorrect.

Imagine if, rather, you employed mindfulness in this circumstance? If you were aware, you would observe that your husband did not finish the errand you requested him, but you would not interpret this behavior or presume that it means something. You would love that you could not understand his motives.

Maybe he had been too busy or too tired. Maybe there were conditions outside his control--for instance, the shop was too far away. Next time you end up making assumptions about a person's actions or goals, be cautious of what you are doing—practice WAIT. Don't forget to ask what occurred and then listen to the truth. Doing this will prevent unnecessary harm, feelings, and abuse to your associations.

Mindfulness of Joy

Recognizing the happiness in your own life--your successes along with the joyful times--can help you handle the difficult times. Noticing just the challenging days, on the flip side, can put you back down and bring about feelings of incapability. To practice in being aware of pleasure, create a list of all of the positive experiences you have had in the previous six weeks.

Maybe you may return within a calendar, your site, or your articles on social media websites to help you recall. You could not be aware of the number of positive experiences you have practically forgotten. Read your list each week, and then add to it as many things as possible. Purposefully doing pleasurable activities is a method of hammering yourself and developing your capacity to deal with anxiety. Here is a casual exercise you may prefer to become accostumed: daily for the next week, then do something which you like, being aware of your own experience. Mindfully drink a cup of great coffee. Mindfully celebrate a birthday. Proceed into a beautiful backyard and leave your camera and phone at home so you can focus your entire attention on everything you smell and see, taking your own time and walking gradually.

Mindfulness of both Location and Action

Being mindful of activity and location means concentrating on where you're and whatever task you are doing at the present time.

So once you're on the job, be cautious of your own work. Concentrate your attention on a single job at one time. Then if you are at home, be at home. Leave work at work. When you are in church, then be church.

When you are driving, maintain the vehicle and just drive. If you do something at one time, you will decrease your anxiety level, and that will raise your capability to handle your emotions.

Indicators That You Are Mindful

Living daily in a mindful manner will reduce your total anxiety. That is not to say it is simple, even for people who practice mindfulness frequently. Getting mindful as you move about your everyday routine can be hard. Among the most difficult facets of mindfulness, especially for mentally sensitive folks, is accepting reality as it is. Be receptive and notice the indicators which singal that you're unaware of something. If you wind up doing such things, it is possible to remind yourself to exercise mindfulness gently.

Wishing

Most of us have fantasies. Some fantasies are modest. For instance, you might wake up one day and say, "I really hope I did not need to go to work now." You may remain in bed that afternoon more than intended and wish you did not need to hurry for work in time. You will finally walk in your cupboard and desire you had an ensemble

99

that matches and then want to lose ten lbs. Other fantasies are big. For instance, lots of individuals sometimes wish that their life scenario was different.

Most of us make fantasies, but wishing can make sure that you remain miserable. Wishing can obstruct taking effective actions, like accepting the situation you are in, learning how to see and enjoy the advantages, or solving an issue by yourself. If you are chronically discontent, you are far more likely to be frustrated if you experience new strain. As soon as you end up wishing that things are different, you challenge yourself. Ask yourself if the circumstance is what you really want or will need to deal with. Maybe you've got a tradition of reacting to minor annoyances by wishing things were different. If it does not actually matter or is outside of your hands, then seek out a different method of tapping it. Perhaps you can practice mindfulness by stating, "That's the moment. Just this instant." You may also state, "Let go, let go" as a means of admitting and releasing unnecessary judgment and upset. "It's exactly what it is" can help.

Complaining

Mindfulness, again, suggests accepting and seeing truth as it is without ruling over it. When you whine, you are not accepting reality as it is. Complaining is a method of stating that scenarios, individuals, and life should be different than they actually are. Complaining is different facing the difficulties When you whine, you are focused on what is wrong instead of what is right with the world. As time passes by, if you whine a lot, you can discover that you are more focused on what you do not like than what you enjoy about your daily life. You might even dismiss the advantages and just concentrate on what isn't good. In this manner, your truth can get jagged, and your distress may grow.

Using "Should"

Another style of never accepting facts is to state that individuals shouldn't do particular things. For instance, you could think your kid shouldn't have stopped her work to marry. Your kid is carrying a higher risk by quitting her job, one probably won't repay her and will probably have unwanted consequences. If that's the circumstance, maybe you are using "should" to point to a safer or better option.

You may also use "should" to signify that something does not match your sense of equity --for instance, kids "shouldn't" have cancer, or else you "shouldn't" have lost those precious, irreplaceable photos of your loved ones. When you state things that do and can occur shouldn't occur, you are not accepting reality as it really is.

Deficiency of approval brings anguish. Perhaps, rather than utilizing "should," you might say you are concerned about the effects of a specific action or which you are miserable and hurt by means of a function.

Preventing

Avoiding difficult situations normally contributes to greater stress and having to survive even more difficult situations afterward. For instance, not visiting this doctor for the fear that something is wrong you might have serious impacts. Preventing somebody who is angry with youvfrom expressing their feelings might cause a reduction in their connection. There are a lot of methods for preventing, and they represent a number of (if not every) ways in which we avoid facing reality. If you are alert, you are going to notice your fear, not let it dominate you.

Awareness of No Acceptance

For daily, or perhaps only an hour notice if you are whining, utilizing "should," preventing, or even wanting things were different. Only notice, then bring yourself back into the current moment and truth. Say something which promotes approval, for example, "I take what I can't change." Keep in mind; approval is not about agreeing with how things are. It's merely an acknowledgment that facts are what it are.

Putting It All Together

The Learning to become aware of your emotions (and also the events which triggered them) will be a crucial ability in emotion direction. Staying at the present time, not estimating, and accepting your emotions are parts of mindfulness training. The next step is to correctly tag exactly what you believe, which can be covered in another chapter.

Chapter #5
Identifying Your Emotions

Although you're born with the capability to experience fundamental emotions, then you did not go into this world knowing the names of these feelings. You heard of tagging your emotions in the exact same manner that you just acquired the significance of different words. For instance, if you created a face and cried, your parent explained to you: "Oh, why are you mad? Perhaps you lost your toy?

I see-- you are unhappy because you can't find your toy. Where can it be? Let us search for this." In the few paragraphs, your parent suspected that your emotion identified the reason behind the emotion, adjusted the suspect, and mimicked problem-solving. This is one way kids learn fundamental emotion administration.

If parents or other caretakers are mentally skillful, the procedure for teaching kids to comprehend body senses and tag them correctly work easily. But many caregivers are sensitive or have difficulty handling their own feelings. Because of this, perhaps nobody in your early life managed to educate you or simulate how to handle emotions efficiently or how to identify emotions in any way. Maybe you were educated to prevent, conceal, or dread your feelings.

How Identifying Your Emotions Helps

There is a physiological reason why understanding what you are feeling is indeed beneficial in handling your own emotions. The amygdala is the area of the brain that initiates the noodle response that will assist you in coping with crises. It behaves without much consideration. If you name your perception, that aids the prefrontal cortex, the executive center of the brain that is accountable for the analytical and logical idea, remain accountable. When you tag an emotion, then you trigger the brain's brake pedal. The articular system informs the amygdala to relax. This helps you not behave impulsively. Along with assisting you not behave impulsively, correctly naming what you feel provides you info. Anger, for instance, generally means there is a problem to address.

If you do not recognize anger or you mislabel it, say, melancholy -- you might not believe that there is a scenario which you want to modify in some manner. The issue would remain exactly the same, along with your distress. If you do not recognize pity, you can believe you do not want to be about folks when you are actually afraid of becoming excluded. You would then further isolate, which could make the problem worse. Being aware of what you are feeling can allow you to link to the reason for the feeling.

If you are unhappy, for instance, you may return to what could have caused you to feel unhappy. Understanding the origin means that you may consider what activities you may take care of to face the issue, get additional details, or take the problem as you cannot change. For instance, perhaps you realize you are unhappy because your friend did not come to a birthday celebration.

You may then let your buddy know you overlooked him. If you mislabel your despair as wrath, then your activities would probably be a lot different. You may quit talking with your buddy or lose your temper with him. That would not help with your despair and may result in losing the friendship, which might have been the initial panic.

Strategies for Identifying Your Emotion

While everybody must deal with difficult emotions, mentally sensitive men and women need the very best emotion control skills they could develop. These skills include understanding body language and tagging your emotions correctly. Learning how to identify your emotions correctly is going to be a giant step in feeling in control.

Assess Your Physical Sensations

If you are not certain what emotion you are experiencing, look closely at your physical occurence. Emotions are thought to be flaws in your system. Stress can be felt at the stomach; anger, at the shoulders, back, and face; and despair, in the torso and possibly the throat. Learn how to comprehend the senses that indicate certain emotions. For instance, you may become exhausted if you are upset or have a hassle when you are anxious. Perhaps you've got an upset stomach when you need to do anything that you dread. If you don't understand when you are undergoing an emotion, being attuned to a physical feedback can allow you to be aware of your own emotions. Everytime, you get a physical feeling in reaction to an external event (for instance, something someone does or says) or which appears strangely. You may want to search for the emotion you'd expect to bring about this occasion and inquire if that is what you are feeling.

What Is Your Body Telling You?

Even if you frequently have difficulty identifying your emotions, even occasionally, it's fairly clear what you are feeling. For instance, once you're watching a sad film, you probably feel unhappy. Practice recognizing what body senses that come together with your emotions in these times. During the next week, if you are feeling sad, mad, hurt, jealous, happy, lonely, guilty, enthusiastic, joyful, or humiliated, see the body senses you have. Write them down to the graph that follows (or even create your own graph). Also, notice body senses, such as headaches, stomach upset, stomachaches, and exhaustion, which you experience in reaction to things that happen or things which people say. Document that information about the graph, too, then figure regarding the emotion.

Emotions	Body Sensations

After completing this exercise, you will probably have a fantastic idea about where on your own body you encounter emotions and may use it as a guide if you are unsure what you are feeling. Obviously, headaches and other pain could be physical in origin; however, physical pain may be aggravated or affected through emotions. If you've got a hassle and you realize you generally get headaches when you are apprehensive, then you're able to search for what may be making you nervous. If you feel despair behind your eyes in your throat, and that is where you are experiencing senses, then you can search for what could have triggered despair.

Analyze Your Urges to Act On Your Emotion

Emotions normally have activities associated with them. The actions you would like to take might provide an idea of what you may feel when you are undergoing an emotion. For instance, the impulse to run away could indicate anxiety. The impulse to hide and prevent eye contact can signify pity—the impulse to attack frequently signals anger.

If you are emotionally sensitive, then you might behave depending on your mood more frequently than other people do. You might be busy with friends and considering the events of this day when you are happy or satisfied but isolate when you are sad or depressed. Additionally, how you see yourself might be commanded by your mood. You might hate yourself if you are hurt or angry, but you could enjoy yourself, or not experiencing such extreme self-dislike, once you're happy.

Although you probably have a strong tendency to behave in your own emotion, really doing this is a selection. If you behave in ways that are consistent with an emotion, then you are likely to raise the strength of the emotion. Consider the sensation that is making you behave in a specific manner: Would you wish to boost this feeling? If not, then alter the activity. Rather than hiding if you are feeling embarrassed, hold your head high, and be sociable. Rather than withdrawing once you are feeling miserable, push to become active and involved. In the majority of scenarios, doing this can help you alter the emotions you are feeling or not raise their strength.

Determine the Reason for Your Emotion

Knowing the reason for your emotion is one more means to identify exactly what you are feeling. When you are trying to find the reason for your psychological experience, consider events that occurred lately, ideas that you are getting, and what you might have felt initially (i.e., main feelings) that led one to feel how you do today. You might find beneficial, to begin with, to keep an eye on circumstances. Although notions can surely cause feelings (as mentioned below), frequently, those ideas were triggered by outside events.

For instance, imagine that you are enjoying breakfast when suddenly you've got an awkward feeling. You then observe that you're considering your ex and identify the exact feeling as despair. You might believe that the ideas of your ex caused despair. On the other hand, the simple fact that you're enjoying a dish which your ex especially liked contributed to ideas on your ex. Then the despair followed the ideas.

So the best reason for your despair was everything you had been searching for breakfast. Think back to what you're doing or thinking about what's occurring when you felt that emotion. At the beginning, you might not recall the facts and think that nothing

110

special happened that may make an emotional reaction. If this is so, proceed through your daily life step by step, at the moment you have got out of bed. For instance, are you currently feeling this emotion once you awakened?

At breakfast? When did you move to the job? During your lunch break? Take a look at everything you did, whatever you've noticed, and what you believed since the previous time you understand you were not feeling the emotion. Consider whom you spoke with and what you spoke about. If you still cannot link your emotion to some occasion, attempt to identify anything which happened in your daily life that will likely make emotion in somebody else. For instance, many individuals would feel frustrated if a buddy told them she could not make it to get a planned film night, as the buddy told you now. Perhaps that is the emotion you are having and could not identify.

A Couple More Options

Another approach for identifying exactly what emotion you are feeling would be to look closely in a record of feelings. You will more readily comprehend your emotion when specified options. Begin with the fundamentals, like pleasure, shock, anger/frustration, shame, guilt, and dread, nervousness, and jealousy.

Proceed through the respective options until you discover a tag that appears to match your expertise. Paying attention to your body language, particularly your facial expression, can do the job also. You might choose to check in the mirror to find out exactly what you're saying communicates. If your face looks gloomy, perhaps that is what you are feeling.

If you have difficulty identifying the emotion carried by your saying, possibly let others inform you about what they see. You can check for any probable causes of the emotion, either to affirm and understand what action is the most appropriate in the circumstance.

You might also look closely at the ideas you are having. If your ideas makes you unhappy, you tend to be experiencing despair. The same is true for different kinds of thoughts. How you think about a specific situation can cause feelings, so being cautious about your thinking can allow you to handle your own emotions. You will find out more about this in another chapter.

Difficulties in Identifying Your Emotions

Knowing exactly what you are feeling is not simple for a lot of factors. Perhaps you don't observe the bodily sensations that go along with your own emotions. Maybe you incorrectly discovered early in life to tag all bodily senses like anger. Perhaps you never heard the names of your emotions in any way, or you also push feelings off for as long as possible, saying you do not feel anything. Perhaps you're confused about your own emotions.

Emotion Confusion

Somebody sensations and feelings can easily be confused, like tiredness and depression or delight and enjoyment. Additionally, psychological reactions may be complicated and occasionally involve numerous emotions and ideas. In certain scenarios, you might mislabel ideas as feelings. Each one of these possibilities will make it difficult to understand what you are feeling. Other feelings that may also be readily confused are anxiety and excitement. With stress, there is a feeling of dread, while delight involves more of a feeling of anticipation.

A trip overseas may result in both excitement and anxiety. So can a brand new, challenging endeavor. If you mislabel enthusiasm as stress, you might opt to steer clear of chances that you would actually appreciate. In the beginning, you may encounter unnecessary distress. Anxiety is sometimes mislabeled also.

Stress is frequently about unpleasant events that may occur later on, typically events over which you don't have any control. For instance, you may feel apprehensive about whether you're going to be hired to get a job that you desire. Stress is all about impending danger, like that somebody may be breaking in your home at the moment. Stress is useful as it makes it possible to take the action that you need to take, like calling 911 or operating out of gunfire, or even anything less pressing but nevertheless significant, like getting to work on time once the boss is questioning those that are late.

Stress based on truth is great for problem solving and security. Stress is useful if it compels you to address an issue or prepare yourself for a future occasion, like practicing for a language or studying for an evaluation. Although maybe not so useful when it is about scenarios where no activity is possible right now or over which you don't have any control. Accurately tagging your emotions can allow you to understand what things to take to handle the circumstance. If you are concerned about maintaining your work, then utilizing that stress to drive yourself to become a much more appreciated employee or to start looking for a different job might be useful. On the flip side, if you are doing everything you can or your problem is outside of your hands, you can use specific methods for handling the signs of stress, such as diversion or relaxing your muscles.

Complex Sensitive Experiences

As mentioned previously, individuals typically encounter numerous emotions simultaneously, but they are occasionally mindful of focusing on just one. For instance, emotionally sensitive individuals often say that they understand that they have a wonderful life; nevertheless, they reside about the one facet that is not going the way they want. Getting mindful of just the one emotion restricts your perspective of your life.

If you are feeling unhappy, you might not observe any happiness that is also current. Perhaps you're mainly miserable, but in precisely the same time, you feel pleasure or gratitude for the loved ones, your house, and your pals. When you truly feel numerous emotions at precisely the same time concerning precisely the same occasion, it can be difficult to tag your emotions correctly. Let's say you are leaving the people that you've worked with for a long time to proceed to a different town.

You are unhappy about leaving your buddies but also joyful, excited, and nervous about the new prospect. Perhaps you have regrets or remorse about previous issues together with your colleagues. It can be tough to pick these emotions aside. Noticing emotions aside from the person who dominates might signify looking for what you're feeling. Doing this can help you remain balanced. You will get a better awareness of your total psychological experience and become overwhelmed by difficult feelings. Completing the subsequent exercise will boost your comprehension of your emotions and provide you to practice tagging your own emotions.

Your Emotional Life

For a single week, pay careful consideration to correctly tagging your own emotions.

Sadness   Anger   Anxiety

Stress   Jealousy   Love

Hurt   Frustration   Joy

Day 1: _____

Day 2: _____

Day 3: _____

Day 4: _____

Day 5: _____

Day 6: _____

Day 7: _____

At the close of the week, review everything you wrote. If you believed any specific emotion most of the time or noticed only a couple of emotions every day, then strive for a different week, appearing even more attentively for more feelings. For instance, if you are anxious, the majority of the time, detect other emotions you have, like minutes of pleasure or flashes of anger. Check-in with yourself regularly to find out what you may be feeling. You might find it beneficial to make a reminder to occasionally know about what you are feeling--for example, by placing your watch to beep every hour.

Combined Ideas and Emotions

Emotions can unite with ideas to make different emotions. For instance, disappointment is ordinarily the result of ideas your expectations were not fulfilled, and feelings of despair. Frustration is a combo of thinking you can address an issue and anger within the difficulty of actually doing this. To put it differently, everything you think might influence your emotions. This will make it difficult to identify the first emotion.

Emotions Can Trigger Other Ideas and Emotions

Occasionally having an emotion about an occasion or a notion concerning an event triggers additional emotions. Maybe you're terrified of feeling depressed. So once you feel unhappy, you become fearful. Or perhaps you don't enjoy feeling depressed, which means you become mad as a means of preventing melancholy. Let's say you are unhappy since your wife lost her job. You become mad to substitute the despair, as you hate feeling depressed --you are feeling less vulnerable once you're mad. When you visit your wife, you talk to her coldly. Perhaps you accuse her of being idle. Then she asserts back and says hurtful things to you. Your activities made the problem worse. Nowadays, you truly feel unhappy. Identifying your primary emotion is essential to working efficiently because that is the emotion that is directly linked to expertise.

Ideas vs. Feelings

If you did the practice "Your Emotional Life," you might have been unsure sometimes what had been a consideration and that which was a sense. Emotionally sensitive individuals frequently confuse the two. For instance, you can frequently say, "I believe" instead of "I presume." Because of this, you might bring feelings to some scenarios where they are not helpful or applicable.

Let's say you are choosing a pioneer to get a workgroup.

Saying "I believe George is a fantastic boss" makes the announcement psychological, even if you rationally assessed George's leadership skills. Additionally, it makes you more inclined to respond emotionally if anybody cares for you. Saying "I believe George is a fantastic leader" requires the announcement from the psychological realm. Expressing thoughts certainly as ideas, not feelings, can enable you to distinguish your emotional reactions from logical thinking.

Some disagreeable thoughts are especially easy to confuse with feelings, and also the confusion makes dealing with them difficult. Imagine your friend shows to others a secret you've shared with her individually. You may say, "I have been betrayed." And you most likely don't have any clue how to manage being betrayed. That is because "betrayed" is not a feeling; it is an idea. To be accurate, you would say, "I understand she's betrayed me." Recognizing in such a manner that "betrayed" is really a consideration will direct you to appropriate actions.

You might opt to take a look at the fact of the scenario or to be cautious about your interactions with this specific friend, or you may choose not to be friends. Your emotions regarding the betrayal are different compared to your ideas. Whenever someone betrays you, then you can feel depressed, upset, or hurt. Identifying how you are feeling will enable you to pick approaches to deal effectively with these feelings.

If you are unhappy, you may opt to comfort yourself. If you are mad, you could give yourself a while to cool before making any conclusions. Both your ideas and feelings of being betrayed are parts of their adventure of being jeopardized and understood. That mix will provide you with a much more precise comprehension of this. Maybe saying "I feel betrayed" is really a shorthand method of seeing that entire expertise, but it does not fully or correctly express your ideas and feelings, which makes dealing with the problem more difficult.

Imagine if you should state "I sense broken"? Much like "betrayed," "busted" is not a sense. Expressing the idea "I am busted" as a sense really masks exactly what you are feeling. To reword the announcement to reflect your emotions and your ideas, you may say, "I believe I am broken as I see myself abandoned by other people." Or even "I sense debilitating despair that tears me apart inside" Identifying your expertise specifically and correctly can assist you to behave with wisdom. You'll also be less inclined to base your opinion on yourself, which might be inaccurate ideas labeled as opinions.

Thought or Feeling?

With this experience, you practice differentiating between feelings and thoughts. Put a checkmark next to all those sentences which are correctly nameable as feelings. Put an X next to all those paragraphs which could be accurately worded. Think about a scenario --maybe one you have really experienced--which may fit the opinion, then imagine how you could reword this sentence.

_____ 1. I'm left out.

_____ 2. I really feel like a failure.

_____ 3. I am pretty.

_____ 4. I need chocolate at the moment.

_____ 5. I'm so jealous I can tear off her head.

_____ 6. I'm confused.

_____ 7. I'm hurt.

_____ 8. I'm disconnected.

_____ 9. I really like potato chips.

_____ 10. I feel clumsy.

Replies

Statements 7 and 5 are all feelings. The rest are ideas. Go back and examine the ones that you missed. For instance, the statement "I really feel like a failure" is an idea mislabeled as a feeling. The feelings which go with believing you are a failure may be despair, grief, humiliation, or shame. See whether it's possible to alter the sentence to say the idea and the feeling(s) individually --for instance, "I believe I fail at all things I do, and then I feel ashamed and sad. I was fired from my job" If this is a true case in the life, it'd be handy to say things this manner instead of "I really feel like a failure," since you can then check the details to check if it was accurate that you fail at all things you do, in addition to addressing the humiliation and despair you accurately expressed.

The Issue of Numbed Infection

It is difficult to identify exactly what you are feeling if you are using foods, other compounds (such as pain tablets), or actions (such as self-harm, overworking, excessive eating, obsessing, or excessive exercise) to purify your emotions. Try to Know about your urges to overeat or too busy yourself with another activity when you are feeling something unfavorable, and consider what emotion you may be having. Exercise letting yourself experience which emotion.

Awareness of The Way You Numb Your Emotions

Pick one behavior you know you utilize to numb unwanted emotions. Some chances are eating, drinking alcohol, and working, utilizing the computer or telephone, excessive busyness, sleeping, interacting, and so forth.

Every time you wish to numb yourself for another week, set a timer for 3 minutes. Just take that opportunity to consider and write down the feelings and ideas which are supporting your impulse. Simply take the entire few minutes, if you're able to, to assist you in understanding emotions which might not be apparent. The feelings and ideas behind your impulse to numb might differ at different times, or you may find you get a consistent routine.

Numbing action: _____

Feelings: _____

Ideas: _____

Feelings: _____

Ideas: _____

Feelings: _____

Ideas: _____

Feelings: _____

Ideas: _____

Feelings: _____

Ideas: _____

Feelings: _____

Ideas: _____

Feelings: _____

Ideas: _____

In performing this workout, perhaps you discovered that the emotion you wished to numb was consistently the same, such as despair; or perhaps you discovered that you wished to numb all feelings. As you proceed, pay special attention to all those feelings you are inclined to prevent. Exercise not numbing those feelings by simply feeling them for an extended time period. Let yourself feel the emotion before it rains. If that is too extreme, then decide on a time period that you're able to handle, for example, five minutes, where you will go through the emotion until deflecting yourself in a wholesome manner, like through physical exercise or speaking with a buddy. You'll come across that the emotion will soon pass. Be aware that if you are conscious of emotion and let yourself experience it, then it is possible to take projected breaks out of it through actions. In this way, you are not preventing the emotion.

Creating False Assumptions or Identifying the Reason for Your Emotion

Whenever people do not understand why they believe what they feel, they might arrive at decisions that look very logical but not accurate. If you are emotionally sensitive, you might be unaware that you could be quite proficient at inventing excuses for your emotions which are not necessarily correct.

At times you might devise reasons for how you are sensitive because, as mentioned, the real causes may be complex, which makes them more difficult to identify. For instance, in certain situations, you might be conscious only of secondary feelings (i.e., the feelings you've got in response to other emotions). Maybe you encounter anger when you feel unhappy, and also, the anger isn't so automatic you're unaware of the despair that arrived. Emotionally sensitive men and women are generally creative. Creative thinking can signify that you make relationships between events that others do not.

The majority of the time, your ability to view and understand the entire world in a different manner is an edge. But there are times when you might see events as applicable even if they are not. You might exaggerate your errors or feature obligation for your events which weren't your fault. You will convince yourself you are accountable for other people's moods and activities. It can be valuable to learn if you've got a knack for viewing events at a self-blaming fashion. Interpreting occasions as your error when they are not adding unnecessary annoyance for your life. To alter this routine, make an effort not to read some concealed significance into others' behaviors or phrases.

If you have ideas about their behavior or words, examine the details of this situation, and receive all of the info before accepting obligation. Becoming clear about the difference between truth and thought is significant in handling feelings. Facts are occasions that you're able to see directly. You can see someone frown; however, you can guess the main reason behind the frown. Just the individual frowning can understand exactly the reason.

When you believe something may be accurate, make certain to inquire instead of making assumptions. However, it is appropriate to understand that your guesses are only guesses. Making assumptions about the others' thoughts as well as the explanations for their behavior frequently generates painful moments. Consider the way you're thinking, maybe strengthening your unwanted

125

emotions. Focusing on thoughts like "She is hoping to have me fired" will increase your stress. Ideas like "he has not returned my phone --he wants to break up with me" can increase your anger, stress, and despair. Just because you've got a notion does not signify that the idea is accurate. Attempt to locate the truth so as not to produce or construct overwhelming emotions according to misinterpretations or untrue assumptions.

For instance, imagine you truly feel stressed but are not certain why. You consider it and realize that a fantastic friend has not contacted you in some time. You think of instances when you may have bothered her. You try to speak to your buddy about why she is angry with you. If she says there is no issue, you do not believe her. You decide there is no way to conserve the connection because she will not speak with you concerning the issue. Thus, hurt and fearful of rejection, so you precede her.

Though you are instinctive, it might be that your buddy is not mad at you. Maybe she is just busy or concerned about something different in her life. You could be right regarding her angry feelings, although not on the rationale for them. Or it might be that your nervousness is not on your friend in any way. Maybe you're uneasy because your kid is moving into another country, and you also worry about her. You do not wish to consider that she is moving, as that is too frightening.

It is less painful to translate your nervousness as needing to do with your buddy being upset with you. If you've got a history of earning false assumptions or incorrectly identifying motives for your emotions, as exemplified previously, you might have stopped expecting to understand why you are feeling how you do. If this is so, then carefully assessing the events which preceded your emotion rather than making assumptions will probably be significant to regaining confidence in your ability to understand your emotions. This worksheet can help you look more carefully at how your feelings influence you.

Your Emotional Habits

During the next week, if you have a psychological response to an event, complete the My Emotions and Behaviour worksheet.

First, clarify the Function. For instance, perhaps your very best friend did not call to wish you on your job interview.

Then list any notions you may have needed --ideas like "She does not care for me, or She has always been covetous; I do not understand why I expected something different."

Next, list the very first emotion you experienced (anger, despair, anxiety, jealousy, happiness, love) then record any emotion resulting in your first emotion. Perhaps you feel anger when you feel despair.

Next, record what info your emotion is providing you. For instance, the hurt may tell you that you appreciate your very best friend's aid. Anger may inform you to problem-solve together with your pal or stand up on your own.

Then write what you really did later with the emotion. Did you overeat? Avoid your buddy? Withdraw?

Ultimately, write the outcomes of your activities, both negative and positive, short term and long-term. Did you find a beautiful new coat and invest too much cash on things you did not require? Did you have a fight with your friend and regret it?

<u>My Emotions and Behaviour</u>

Truth: _____

Trigger ideas: _____

Initial emotion: _____ Secondly Awareness: _____

Info: _____

Action: _____

Outcomes (short term and long term): _____

Whenever you've got a week's of advice, look over everything you wrote. Assess for psychological patterns. Maybe you normally go shopping for those who are feeling unhappy or blame yourself if somebody's angry. Perhaps once you think mean thoughts on your own, you are inclined to feel mad or depressed. If that is how it is, find out ways to alter the design. Maybe what attracts your feelings is something you are able to alter. Perhaps waking to filthy dishes brings the notion that you are a lazy slob, that causes hopelessness, which contributes to keep you at home or become active at all. The long term effects would be that you don't create progress toward targets which are important for you, like taking courses or gaining friends. Not having dirty dishes awaiting you in the morning can change your disposition.

Putting It All Together

Correctly identifying your emotions is essential for emotion administration. This goes for anybody. If you are emotionally sensitive, then it is even more crucial that you understand and fortify the means by which you'll be able to deal with your feelings, as your emotions could be so extreme. When you're proficient at utilizing the strategies you have learned in this phase to identify your own emotions and triggers, knowing the best way to react to specific emotions can allow you to effectively deal with them. In subsequent chapters, you will find out different methods of altering your psychological patterns. For instance, in another chapter, you will know about letting go of conclusions on your own, other people, and the planet, that are inclined to improve your feelings and make you more inclined to be overwhelmed with your own psychological experiences.

Chapter #6
Developing Your Identity

Many mentally sensitive men and women are often unsure about what it really means to be aware of individuality or how to create one. Your private identity (i.e., your awareness of who you have on your side, or your own self-view) comprises the identifying, enduring traits which are a part of your character, like your psychological sensitivity.

It partly depends on the various social functions you undoubtedly occupy--like spouse, dad, brother, and friend. It might also partly depend on the culture and groups that you belong to, for example, middle class and also Irish. Values and morals that guide your decisions in life, your passions, and your career dreams are part of your individuality too. Creating a good sense of individuality will prevent you from being overwhelmed by your own emotions.

When you've got a feeling of who you are, your psychological reactions--especially your responses to social difficulties--will probably be less frequent and extreme. You will be less inclined to observe others' conclusions and responses as risks or as defining your values. You will not be fearful of being rejected or abandoned. You will also be less inclined to conceal your emotions or be embarrassed by your psychological reactions. Making conclusions won't be as overwhelming since you are going to be clear about what is important for you. An erroneous or shaky awareness of individuality can manifest in different ways.

You might choose other people's struggles and feelings, not able to distinguish their encounters from yours. You might end up becoming mad or profoundly sad by simply talking with somebody who's feeling like that. Additionally, you could make choices which are logical, but do not match your character or do not do the job well in the long term. You'll make many wrong moves down the several avenues of life, feeling as you hadn't a map to orient. Your opinion of yourself might depend too much on how others see you. Maybe you judge and establish yourself as faulty rather than ordinary to the stage you despise yourself.

Recognizing Your Identity Development

Your identity does not come to you completely developed. You understand who you're from your adventures over the years; to a point, your individuality is evolving. As a youngster, you started to create awareness of yourself through the consciousness of what you likes, dislikes, your abilities, and how others consider you. But emotionally sensitive kids frequently don't receive precise feedback about themselves since their caregivers do not know their significance or do not possess the abilities, like the capability to comprehend the difficulty of particular tasks and scenarios in order to offer true opinions.

Perhaps your beloved families and friends were ashamed of your emotions so they invited you in one manner or the other to conceal them. Perhaps you're told you could not possibly be as mad as you seem or that you're only attempting to find your way. Maybe your feelings have been ignored. The comments you received might have been so damaging that you just came to see your actual self as improper. Perhaps you had been told that you're overly emotional, too feeble, too destitute, or just "mad." But today, you might be scared of understanding yourself or encounter such pity about who you feel you're to the point that it is painful to consider doing it. Just take a deep breath, and let us look at exactly what is and is not accurate about who you're.

Myths vs. Facts About Who You Are

You might have grown up together with different people's perspectives of your behavior or personality ingrained in your mind. You might not even be conscious that some ideas you have about yourself initially came from different people and don't have any foundation in reality.

If you find yourself as a waste of space, perhaps that thought came from professionals or significant individuals in your life who'd little to donate or were overrun by their lives. Perhaps, in other words, that opinion was about themselves, then it had been all about you. Maybe your loved ones thought that revealing emotions meant you're feeble or that not obtaining a fantastic grade meant that you're dumb.

Every household has its own problems, and these misperceptions are typical. Myths can also come out of your own experiences. For instance, if you were not proficient in softball or football when you're a kid, you might have determined you don't have the capability to perform any bodily tasks nicely.

If your household were athletes that might have contributed to additional negative truths about yourself, like that you do not understand the way to have fun. While it's true you were not a soccer player, you may have performed well in other bodily pursuits. Perhaps you were not athletic but had pleasure in different ways.

Identifying Myths About Who You Are

Put a checkmark in the area next to some of the subsequent statements which you concur with. At the close of the listing, compose some other negative beliefs that you have about yourself.

1. _____ I am a burden to other people.

2. _____ I am a flawed human being, and I cannot let others understand or I will be cast from society.

3. _____ If I talk for myself, then I will be lonely.

4. _____ I always have to put other things first. That is my purpose.

5. _____ I really don't fit in society.

6. _____ I want a person to take good care of me emotionally.

7. _____ I must maintain a romantic relationship or I cannot survive.

8. _____ I am weak because I've extreme feelings.

All of these are myths. From the exercises to come, you practice developing these truths to reality.

Changing Truth About Who You Are

Your beliefs about your self-influence are about how you live your life. So long as your beliefs are true, they allow you to make decisions concerning what scenarios will be useful, comprehend what conditions may be hard, predict how individuals will respond to you, and ascertain what actions you may like. If your beliefs in yourself are not true, you could be perplexed by the way other men and women see you. Deficiency of useful understanding on your own makes it more challenging to handle your emotions. People generally have a propensity to see just the evidence that supports their faith and dismiss some proof to the contrary. That is one reason why we frequently continue to take misconceptions.

Debunking Your Truth

Employing the myths which you marked from the exercise above, try out a test. Actively look for info that tells you precisely the reverse of everything you think. If you marked that the very first myth, as an instance, start looking for ways to convince yourself that you are not a burden on other people. Think hard and frankly about it, and do not dismiss yourself. Consider what you bring to others' lives. Ask folks that you anticipate what they think.

If you marked dream 3, 2, 7, 7, or 8, then start looking for cases among men and women in the information or on your community which may disprove this fantasy --lots of individuals have confessed their defects without even being shunned by society. Now go back and reword the truths to reflect the facts and give you more precise awareness of yourself. For instance, "I must maintain a romantic relationship or that I cannot live" may be reworded into "I need to be in a romantic relationship so badly that occasionally I believe I cannot survive without it." Keep in mind that accepting that fact does not mean that you're committing, settling, or even working out any less to lower your pain and have exactly what you would like in life.

Occasionally myths or false beliefs about yourself derive from older behaviors. Maybe when you're younger, you acted impulsively and also did things you despised, like running away or exploding. Maybe now you are more cautious about your choices and do not take part in these spontaneous behaviors. If you still think about yourself as somebody who's spontaneous even though you don't behave this way, then your opinion of yourself is currently out of date. Think about the myths which you identified previously. Are some of these myths based on your past rather than on the current?

You could also have myths about yourself, which derive from a single or two isolated events. Though you might have lied about your actions to your boyfriend a couple of decades back, there is no reason to find yourself like a liar if you have not repeated that behavior consistently in your relationships. Simultaneously, the majority of individuals have patterns of behavior they aren't proud of that have adverse consequences. If you generally participate in these behaviors, then shifting those damaging patterns is vital. Use the following exercise to think about patterns of unhelpful behavior that reveal ways you see yourself, which influence your decisions and choices.

Your Story

Write out a description of the significant events in your life during recent years. Contain significant errors, successes, along with life events and things you've learned in everyday experience. Illustrate your flaws and strengths. Consider the general subject of your life. Potential topics are beating challenges, loss, survival, empowerment, empathy, shame, battle, chaos, achievement, endurance, and devotion.

Go over everything you have composed, highlighting any routines that you see. The routines will probably be regarding the theme. In your narrative, what job would you have? Have you been the enthusiast? The protagonist? The sufferer? Are you currently the star of your story, or is somebody else the most important focus?

If you are not the celebrity or enthusiast, rewrite your story in the viewpoint where you are while sticking to reality. How can you endure tough scenarios? Make the topic of the narrative a favorable one. How can it be different? Maybe the psychological tone of the narrative changes or how you explain yourself is different. Perhaps you notice results you did not see previously. If you fight to locate a way to rewrite the narrative, it could be because myths regarding your function in life are becoming a part of your core beliefs about yourself, and it is difficult to find the narrative in any other manner. In cases like this, ask a trusted friend to aid you rewriting it. Keep in mind that the narrative does not have to switch to some nice person --you simply would like to represent whatever strengths and advantages were obvious in you or grown because of this.

Stereotypes

Another method of knowing the ability of the other's beliefs about your behavior is via the research which was performed about stereotypes. Stereotypes are similar to myths. A whole lot of individuals think about people with a common trait or a specific method of doing things. From the 1960s, Robert Rosenthal and Lenore Jacobson (1963) administered an assessment to all students in a basic school. Then they told the educators who, according to the evaluation results, some pupils were especially likely to excel in the approaching calendar year, whereas others were not.

The pupils identified as "gifted" were picked randomly, not by their performance on the evaluation. In the conclusion of the calendar year, nevertheless, these students scored significantly higher on an IQ test compared to other pupils. That is a wonderful outcome. The pupils themselves did not understand they were designated as substantial achievers, and neither did their parents. Just the teachers understood. Hence the investigators reasoned the instructors' expectations induced the teachers to behave in a way that enhanced the operation of the pupils who'd been tagged as vivid. Other people's expectations influence both how they treat you and how you act. Stereotypes are a sort of expectancy.

Generally, the stereotype of mentally sensitive individuals is they're wimpy, touchy-feely, shaky, weak, undependable, a pushover, over-reactive, higher care, and less professional than people that aren't seen as emotionally sensitive. This stereotype may impact how you see yourself, in addition to your performance in scenarios where others have that opinion of you.

Any moment you believe you're being judged with the sensitive stereotype, then you could possibly be terrified of showing "a lot of" emotion, that could have adverse implications for your relationships or your livelihood. Guarding against feelings takes away from you power and concentration you need to dedicate to your project or into the people that you're interacting with. The additional tension in fear of being tagged will help it become more difficult to handle your emotions. The longer you care, the more frustrated you're going to be. The greater the stakes to your operation, the more panicked you will probably be.

You will go to work every day decided not to show emotion and be fearful of other people, tagging you negatively. Maybe sometimes you'll be so fearful that you'll shout, maybe because you are mad at somebody. You fear that if you shout, you are going to be judged as too unprofessional or feeble.

Your anxieties and fears make your task more exhausting and difficult. Because of this, you are actually more inclined to shout. If it goes on for quite a while, you might see yourself as a competent employee, and your capacity to perform your work well will reduce.

Perhaps you are not certain what would occur if you yelled at the office, however, the anxiety is still there. Even if you're unsure that whatever negative could occur if you're tagged "emotionally sensitive," you simply need to feel that something negative may occur.

So what do you do? In scenarios where you are concerned about being stereotyped by your emotional sensitivity, then you might choose to hold up your head and say, "Yes, I am emotionally sensitive; therefore, I will be back once I wipe a few tears off." Or you may use humor to defuse the circumstance, like grinning and saying, "No, I am overly emotionally sensitive to see animations, not as much reality shows." If you are familiar with your sensitivity, then many others are somewhat more inclined to accept it too. Practice accepting yourself when others do not.

Roles That Keep You Allergic

The roles that you occupy compared to other men and women are a part of your individuality. You most likely have the role in your family and with your friends as "the mentally sensitive." More specifically, you might be viewed as "the affectionate person," "the loving one," or even "the person who will always assist." You could also be "that the person who overreacts" or even "the person who's too brittle to listen to bad news."

141

No matter what your roles is, your role affects your individuality. Whenever your family expects you to respond in certain ways, there is normally a powerful pull to do exactly that. Additionally, your function will influence others to treat you. If you are "the listener," others might not understand that occasionally you'd love to speak too. If you are viewed as too brittle, others might keep secrets from you personally or even never tell you the truth.

If they view you as "the silent one," they might not request your input. Your relatives and friends might not truly hear your concerns or hurt feelings, even attributing all of your negative psychological reactions to your psychological sensitivity, even if your responses will be just like those that aren't emotionally sensitive. Rather than saying, "I am sorry you are angry about your buddy's behavior," for instance, somebody might ask, "You are not going all play queen again, are you?" This is unjust, to say the very least; however, it's possible to do something about it.

Redefining Your Roles

To know more about the way others' expectations influence your behavior, write a description of your role according to your loved ones. You can write it in a diary or notebook, or even just on another sheet of newspaper. Then write a description of your role concerning your closest buddies. Make sure to add how your behavior results in the role you've got. How can your role affect your connection with every single individual? What do you like about your character, and which does not work for you personally?

Read what you've written. Write what you'd love to change in your character with your loved ones and your character with friends and family. How do you have to behave differently to modify your role?

For instance, let us say you would like to be regarded as somebody who will listen without getting angry. You would like to modify your character with friends and family from becoming "the man or woman who overreacts" to "somebody who is a fantastic listener."

You understand that if people speak with you about their problems, you tend to get anxious, worry about all of the horrible things that may lead to, then judge yourself. Your strategy may include things like practicing relaxation exercises to reduce your stress. Practicing mindfulness daily might help you remain in the moment and not think about horrible things that may occur. You might also practice careful listening and not judging.

Create a blueprint for how to modify your role. Pick just a couple of adjustments to make at one moment. List specifically what abilities you will use to act in a new way.

Track your progress. This might be as straightforward as checking off if you practiced a talent, for example, careful listening, in your calendar every day. Reward yourself for practice, including a glow for persevering. You are able to add more abilities to exercise as you grow gradually. Even though it might take a while, folks will notice the changes you are making and see you in a brand new manner. When they perform, their expectations may change, and you're going to discover that it's simpler to work with your new abilities.

Emptiness and Identity

Not everybody who is emotionally sensitive feels emptiness in regard to their individuality, while other people might not experience it the same way. One mentally sensitive individual clarified emptiness as being "just like a cold shell," a shell of an individual who has no insides, nothing. It seems just like you can't breathe, and you've nowhere to really go for refuge. Suffocating.

Another mentally sensitive individual clarified emptiness as not understanding how you feel, or not understanding what you need in life, leaving one with a dim, empty gap, particularly in the gut and head. Emptiness is emptiness. Nothing seems to exist and you do not know exactly what you believe; if you can even sense anything at the first location.

It absorbs you, and nothing and nobody will fill that emptiness. The emptiness of individuality appears to be not understanding exactly who you are, what you believe, or whatever you would like to be. It is a sense of hollow, a nothingness. It is as if you're a puppet simply responding to what is expected from you to do depending on which rope is pulled. There is distress in emptiness, which leads some individuals to look for pain. Other folks attempt to satisfy the emptiness with alcohol, drugs, food, work, or other compulsive behavior.

Some become too dependent on someone else. In reality, many who undergo emptiness of individuality find some relaxation by being about others and carrying to a pseudo-identity that is suitable for the group they are with. If you have a tendency to do this, you might fear that whenever you aren't with people, the emptiness remains apparent, and you have again the feeling of uncertainty about how to behave and which person to be. Filling the emptiness entails establishing your identity, discovering significance, donating, and linking with life and with other individuals.

Mindfulness is a way to start. During mindfulness, you can concentrate on existing and creating a feeling of your thoughts and tastes by paying more attention to your ideas and feelings. What is your favorite color? Which restaurant do you like to have dinner with friends? How would you decide to spend a free day if you can do anything you wanted? Hurry to discover answers to those questions if you do not know them.

Try different hobbies to find out the way you enjoy spending your own time. Allocate some time into contemplating your spirituality. What should you think? Perhaps you'd love to find out more about different religious philosophies. Look closely at your worth in life.

Which is your biggest gift? Practice naming three different things you are thankful for every day to help identify what you really appreciate.

Be conscious of the means by which you contribute to other people. Perhaps you're a fantastic listener, or perhaps you cheer up people along with your gift of comedy. Maybe you frequently help others overcome barriers, or you also easily provide compassion and love. Perhaps those behaviors point to exactly what you appreciate. If your addiction is to try to conceal out of the emptiness by simply being with other people, do something alone. Let yourself spend short amounts of time tolerating the distress which you'll initially sense. Working to take and fill out the emptiness instead of preventing it. With time, it will result in a peaceful and satisfying life.

Putting It All Together

Problems with identity appear to abound for mentally sensitive individuals. Hopefully, by putting the ideas within this chapter to practice, you have already started to locate your identity, getting more stable and transparent. Now that you have a more precise and secure sense of your individuality and abilities to handle intense feelings, you are all set to check at building and enhancing relationships. Creating and maintaining supportive relationships will probably prove to be quite helpful in those instances as soon as your emotions threaten to overwhelm you.